Collins Primary

Contents

Globes

Globes are models of the Earth. They show the true shape and size of the continents.

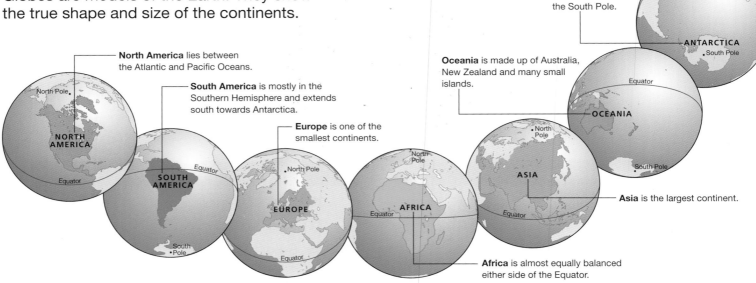

North America lies between the Atlantic and Pacific Oceans.

South America is mostly in the Southern Hemisphere and extends south towards Antarctica.

Europe is one of the smallest continents.

Antarctica encircles the South Pole.

Oceania is made up of Australia, New Zealand and many small islands.

Asia is the largest continent.

Africa is almost equally balanced either side of the Equator.

Map projections

To show the world on a flat map we need to peel the surface of the globe and flatten it out. There are many different methods of altering the shape of the Earth so that it can be mapped on an atlas page. These methods are called **projections**.

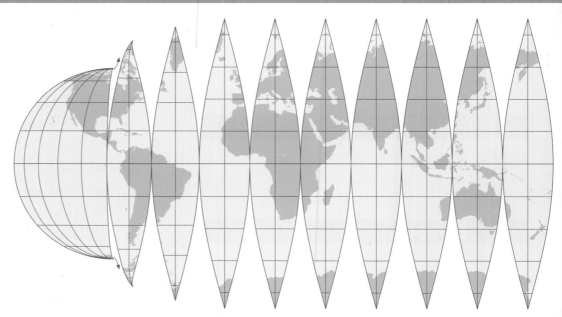

This is how the Earth would look if the surface could be peeled and laid flat.

Map projections change the shape and size of the continents and oceans. The projection used for world maps in this atlas is called Eckert IV.

How the world map looks, depends on which continents are at the centre of the map. Compare the shape of Africa on the maps below to that on the globe.

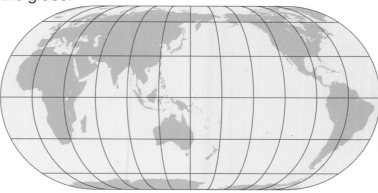

For UK atlases the world would look like this.

For Australian atlases the world would look like this.

Latitude and longitude

We use latitude and longitude to locate places on the Earth's surface. Lines of **latitude** are imaginary lines. They are numbered in degrees North or South of the Equator.

Lines of **longitude** are imaginary lines which run from the North to the South Poles. They are numbered in degrees East or West of a line through London known as the Greenwich Meridian.

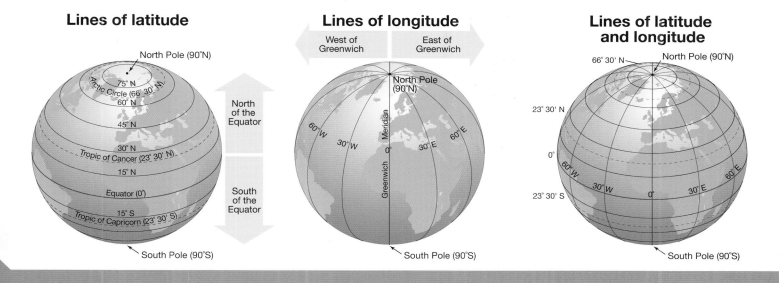

Lines of latitude

Lines of longitude

Lines of latitude and longitude

Hemispheres

The Equator divides the globe into two halves. All land north of the Equator is called the Northern Hemisphere. Land south of the Equator is called the Southern Hemisphere. 0° and 180° lines of longitude also divide the globes into two imaginary halves, the Western and Eastern Hemispheres.

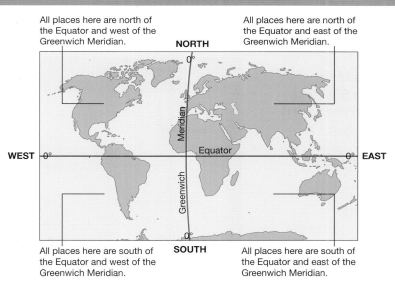

Grid references

As well as using lines of latitude and longitude to find places, this atlas uses grids. The columns are labelled with a letter and the rows with a number. The grid code (e.g. B6) can be used to find all places within one grid square.

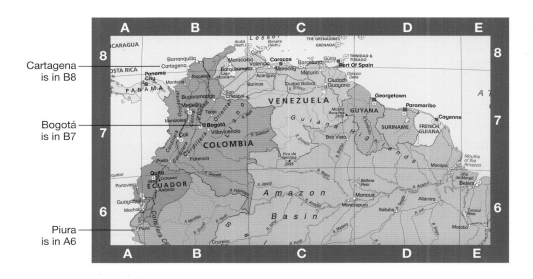

Cartagena is in B8

Bogotá is in B7

Piura is in A6

Atlas maps

Atlas maps help us to find out what places are like.
They tell us about different environments in the world.

Some maps show
country shapes and
where towns are
located within the
country. These are
called political maps.

Some maps show
landscapes. They
show the physical
environment.

Understanding maps

Special names and numbers are used to label parts of an atlas map.

Page number
This helps you to find out
where the map you want is
in the atlas.

Locator map
This shows the part of the
world covered by the map.

Key
This explains what the colours
and symbols used on the
map represent.

Scale
This explains how large a
map is. It helps to work out
distances between places.
See page 6 to find out more
about scale.

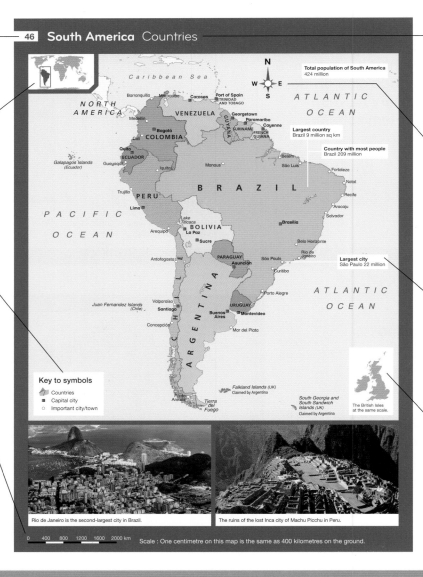

Title
This names the map
area and describes
what the map shows.

Compass
This always points
north-south on the map.
It shows east and west.
Other directions can be
found from the compass.

Fact boxes
These contain interesting
information about a
continent.

Area comparison
This map shows the
size of the British Isles
compared to the region
mapped.

Map symbols

Maps are made up of symbols and names. The symbols can be points, lines or area colours.
A map is complete when the symbols and the names are combined.

Point symbols

■ ○ Town stamps
▲ Mountain peaks
⊕ Airports

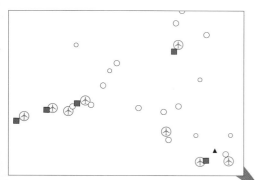

Point symbols are used on a map to show towns, mountain peaks and airports.

Lines

——— Roads
╫╫╫╫ Railways
——— Rivers
——— Coastline

Lines are used on a map to show communications and drainage.

Area colours

Lake/sea
Country colours

Area colours are used to distinguish one country from another and the land from the sea.

Names on atlas maps

The style and size of the type used on maps helps to explain what the name means.

Large bodies of water

PACIFIC OCEAN
Gulf of Guinea

Islands

Cuba
Bioko

Countries

N I G E R I A
BENIN

Large cities

Porto-Novo
Lomé

Small towns

Parakou
Makurdi

Rivers

R. Mississippi
R. Nile
R. Amazon

Mountain peaks

Mount Cameroon
Mount Everest

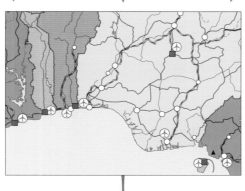

All the symbols are combined to show features and their correct locations.

Names are needed to show places and features shown on the map. Only some places and features are named.

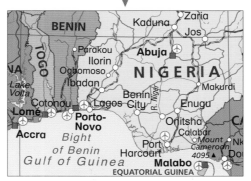

The map is complete when the symbols and the names are combined.

Scale

Maps are much smaller than the regions they show. To compare the real area with the mapped area you have to use a scale. Each map in this atlas shows its scale. This is shown using a scale bar which is explained in words.

E.g.
0   200   400   600   800 km

Scale : One centimetre on this map is the same as 200 kilometres on the ground.

Large scale

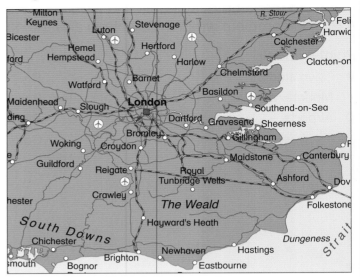

Scale : One centimetre on this map is the same as 20 kilometres on the ground.

0   20   40   60   80   100 km

Large scale maps show smaller areas with more detail. ⬅

Measuring distance

The scale of a map can be used to measure how far it is between two places. For example, the straight line distance between Boa Vista and Cayenne on the map to the right is 5 centimetres.

Look at the ruler.
One centimetre on this map is the same as 200 kilometres on the ground. The real distance between Boa Vista and Cayenne is therefore 1000 kilometres (i.e. 5 x 200).

0   200   400   600   800 km   Scale : One centimetre on

Medium scale

Scale : One centimetre on this map is the same as
250 kilometres on the ground.

0   250   500   750   1000   1250 km

Small scale

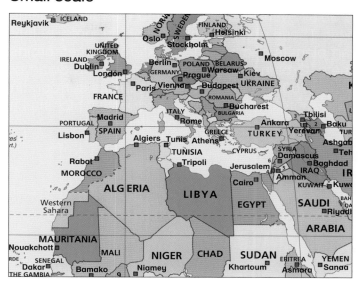

Scale : One centimetre on this map is the same as
800 kilometres on the ground.

0   800   1600   2400   3200 km

Small scale maps show larger areas with less detail.

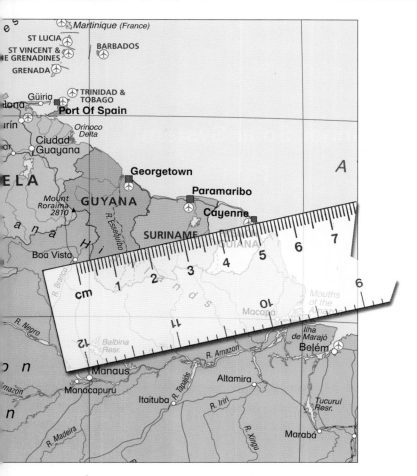

is the same as 200 kilometres on the ground.

Finding directions

Directions help you to work out which way to go when you travel from place to place. There are four main compass directions: North (N), East (E), South (S) and West (W). These are called the cardinal points. The compass can also be divided in eight points as shown in the diagram below.

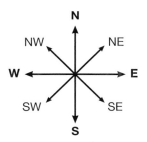

An eight-point compass

The needle of the compass always points to the north because it is magnetic. Maps are usually drawn to match the compass with north at the top and south at the bottom.

The Solar System

The Solar System is the Sun and the many objects that orbit it. These objects include eight planets, at least five dwarf planets and countless asteroids, meteoroids and comets. Orbiting some of the planets and dwarf planets are over 160 moons. The Sun keeps its surrounding objects in its orbit by its pull of gravity which has an influence for many millions of kilometres.

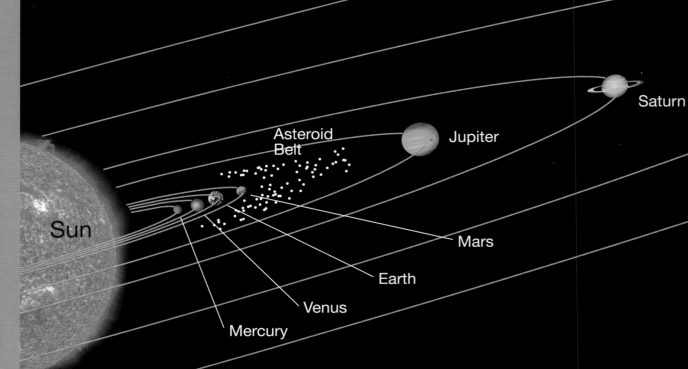

Saturn

Asteroid Belt

Jupiter

Sun

Mars

Earth

Venus

Mercury

Planets of the Inner Solar System

PLANET →	Mercury	Venus	Earth	Mars
DISTANCE → (from the Sun)	58 million kilometres	108 million kilometres	150 million kilometres	228 million kilometres

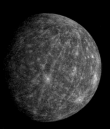

Mercury is the smallest planet and closest to the Sun.

Venus lies between Earth and the Sun. It is the brightest object in the sky.

Earth is the only planet in the Universe known to support life. Most of its surface is covered in water.

Mars is known as the red planet. It has a mountain which rises 24 kilometres above the land.

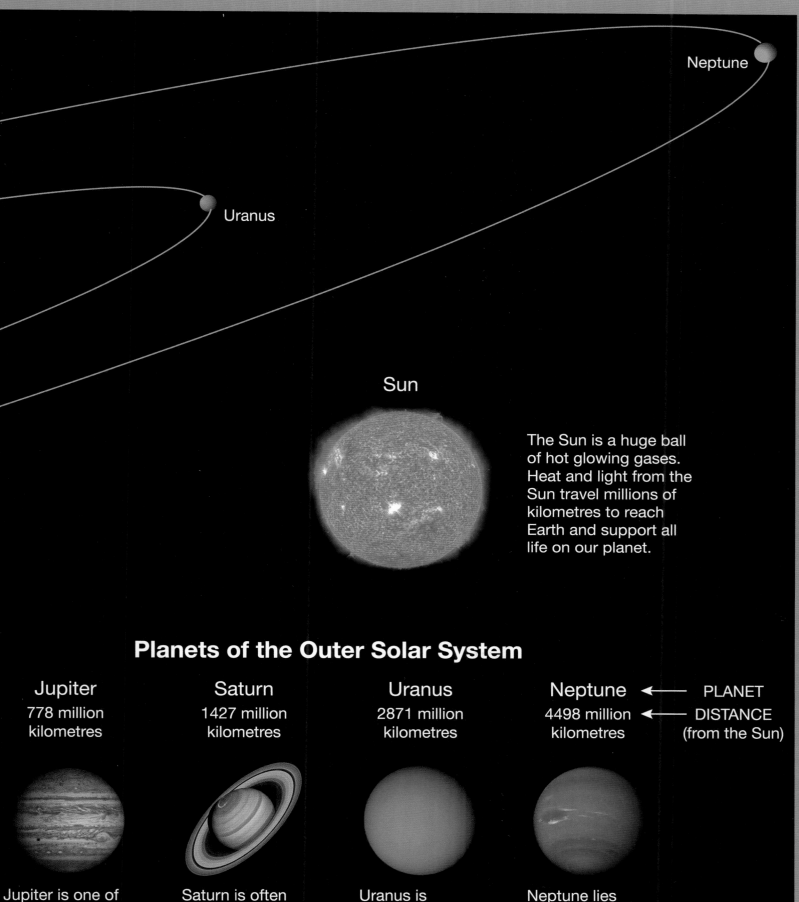

Neptune

Uranus

Sun

The Sun is a huge ball of hot glowing gases. Heat and light from the Sun travel millions of kilometres to reach Earth and support all life on our planet.

Planets of the Outer Solar System

Jupiter	Saturn	Uranus	Neptune ← PLANET
778 million kilometres	1427 million kilometres	2871 million kilometres	4498 million kilometres ← DISTANCE (from the Sun)

Jupiter is one of the giant planets. It is more than 300 times bigger than Earth.

Saturn is often called the 'ringed planet' because it is surrounded by rings of dust and rocks.

Uranus is known as the 'blue planet'. It orbits the Sun on its side.

Neptune lies furthest from the Sun, and is the windiest planet in the Solar System.

The Moon

Only one side of the Moon is visible from Earth, the far side has only been seen by the few astronauts whose spaceships orbited it in the late 1960s and early 1970s.

Earth and its Moon compared

Plato

Mare Imbrium (Sea of Rains)

Montes Apeninus

Mare Serenitatis (Sea of Serenity)

Oceanus Procellarum (Ocean of Storms)

Copernicus

Mare Tranquillitatis (Sea of Tranquility)

● *Apollo 11 landing site (first men on the Moon)*

Mare Nubium (Sea of Clouds)

Tycho

The phases of the Moon

| New moon | Waxing crescent | First quarter | Waxing gibbous | Full moon | Waning gibbous | Last quarter | Waning crescent | New moon |

The new moon is not visible from Earth

The seasons

The Earth's axis is tilted from perpendicular therefore different parts of the globe are oriented towards the Sun at different times of the year. The four seasons, Spring, Summer, Autumn and Winter are a result of this.

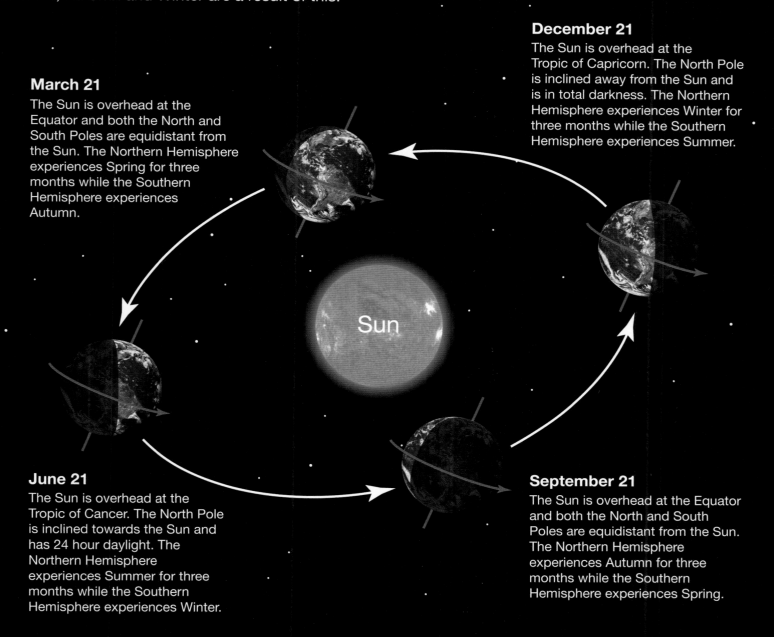

December 21

The Sun is overhead at the Tropic of Capricorn. The North Pole is inclined away from the Sun and is in total darkness. The Northern Hemisphere experiences Winter for three months while the Southern Hemisphere experiences Summer.

March 21

The Sun is overhead at the Equator and both the North and South Poles are equidistant from the Sun. The Northern Hemisphere experiences Spring for three months while the Southern Hemisphere experiences Autumn.

June 21

The Sun is overhead at the Tropic of Cancer. The North Pole is inclined towards the Sun and has 24 hour daylight. The Northern Hemisphere experiences Summer for three months while the Southern Hemisphere experiences Winter.

September 21

The Sun is overhead at the Equator and both the North and South Poles are equidistant from the Sun. The Northern Hemisphere experiences Autumn for three months while the Southern Hemisphere experiences Spring.

Sun

Day and night

The Earth rotates on its axis every 24 hours. At any moment in time one side of the Earth is in sunlight, while the other half is in darkness.

Direction of rotation

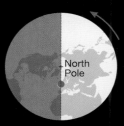

Dawn in the UK

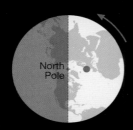

Midday in the UK

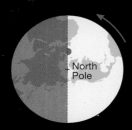

Dusk in the UK

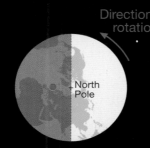

Midnight in the UK

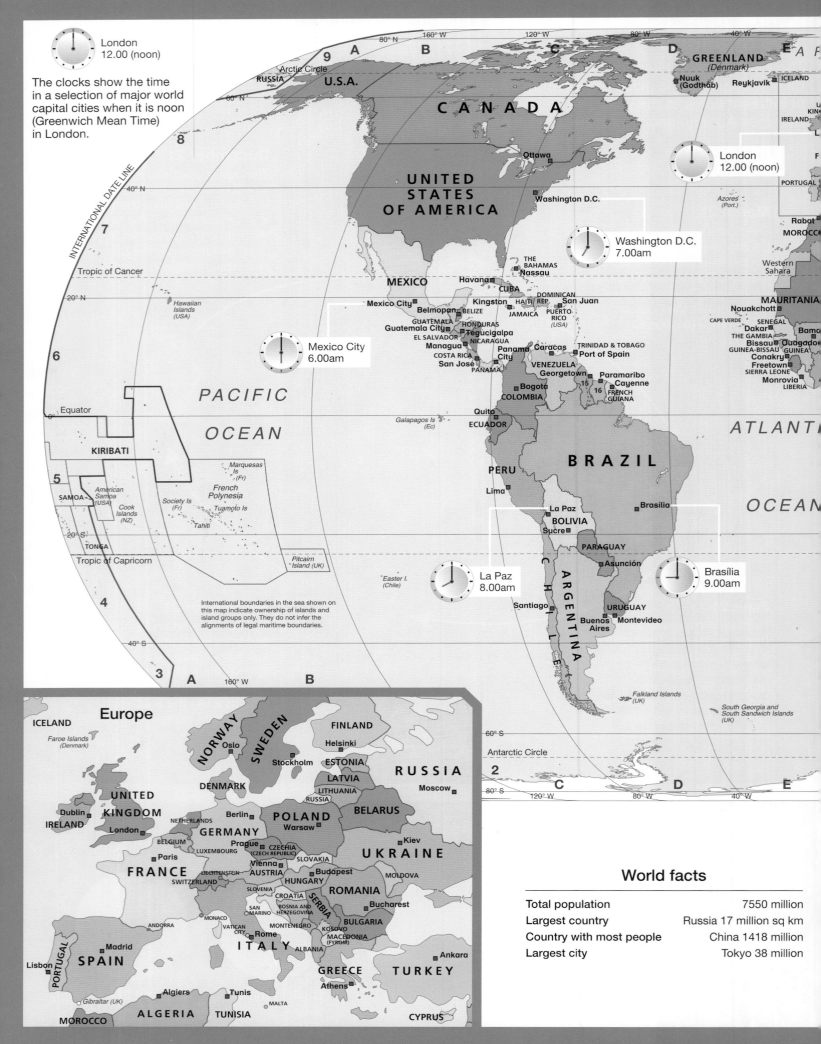

London
12.00 (noon)

The clocks show the time in a selection of major world capital cities when it is noon (Greenwich Mean Time) in London.

INTERNATIONAL DATE LINE

80° N   160° W   120° W   80° W   40° W

9 A   B   C   D   GREENLAND
(Denmark)   E A R

Arctic Circle
RUSSIA   U.S.A.   Nuuk
(Godthåb)   Reykjavik   ICELAND

60° N

CANADA   U
KIN

8   IRELAND

40° N   UNITED
STATES
OF AMERICA   Ottawa   London
12.00 (noon)   PORTUGAL

7   Washington D.C.   Azores
(Port.)   Rabat
MOROCCO

Washington D.C.
7.00am   Western
Sahara

Tropic of Cancer   THE
BAHAMAS
Nassau   MAURITANIA

20° N   MEXICO   Havana   Nouakchott
Hawaiian
Islands
(USA)   CUBA   CAPE VERDE   SENEGAL
Mexico City   Kingston   DOMINICAN
REP.   San Juan   Dakar   Bama
Belmopan   HAITI   THE GAMBIA   Ouagadou
Mexico City
6.00am   BELIZE   PUERTO   Bissau
GUATEMALA   HONDURAS   RICO   GUINEA-BISSAU   GUINEA
Guatemala City   Tegucigalpa   (USA)   Conakry
EL SALVADOR   NICARAGUA   Freetown
Managua   Caracas   SIERRA LEONE   Monrovia
COSTA RICA   Panama   TRINIDAD & TOBAGO   LIBERIA
San José   City   Port of Spain
PANAMA   VENEZUELA
Georgetown   Paramaribo
15   Cayenne
Bogotá   16   FRENCH
COLOMBIA   GUIANA

6

PACIFIC   Quito
ECUADOR

Equator   Galapagos Is
(Ec)

OCEAN   ATLANTI

KIRIBATI   BRAZIL

PERU   OCEAN

Marquesas
Is
(Fr)   Lima   Brasília
5   French
Polynesia   La Paz
SAMOA   American
Samoa
(USA)   Society Is
(Fr)   Tuamoto Is   BOLIVIA
Sucre
Cook
Islands
(NZ)   Tahiti   PARAGUAY

20° S   TONGA   Asunción   Brasília
9.00am
Tropic of Capricorn   Pitcairn
Island (UK)   La Paz
8.00am   A
R   C   Easter I.
(Chile)   La Paz   G   H
International boundaries in the sea shown on
this map indicate ownership of islands and
island groups only. They do not infer the
alignments of legal maritime boundaries.   E   I
N   L
Santiago   T   E
4   I
N   URUGUAY
40° S   Buenos   Montevideo
Aires

3   A   B
160° W   Falkland Islands
(UK)   South Georgia and
South Sandwich Islands
(UK)

60° S   Antarctic Circle

2   C   D   E

80° S
120° W   80° W   40° W

Europe

ICELAND   NORWAY   SWEDEN   FINLAND
Faroe Islands
(Denmark)   Oslo   Helsinki

Stockholm   ESTONIA   RUSSIA
LATVIA
DENMARK   LITHUANIA   Moscow
UNITED   RUSSIA
Dublin   KINGDOM   NETHERLANDS   Berlin   POLAND   BELARUS
IRELAND   London   GERMANY   Warsaw
BELGIUM   Prague   Kiev
LUXEMBOURG   CZECHIA
(CZECH REPUBLIC)   UKRAINE
Paris   LIECHTENSTEIN   Vienna   SLOVAKIA
FRANCE   AUSTRIA   Budapest   MOLDOVA
SWITZERLAND   SLOVENIA   HUNGARY   ROMANIA
SAN   CROATIA   Bucharest
MARINO   BOSNIA AND   SERBIA
ANDORRA   MONACO   HERZEGOVINA   BULGARIA
VATICAN   MONTENEGRO   KOSOVO
CITY   Rome   MACEDONIA
Madrid   (FYROM)   Ankara
Lisbon   ITALY   ALBANIA
SPAIN   GREECE   TURKEY
Gibraltar (UK)   Algiers   Tunis   Athens
MALTA
MOROCCO   ALGERIA   TUNISIA   CYPRUS

World facts

Total population	7550 million
Largest country	Russia 17 million sq km
Country with most people	China 1418 million
Largest city	Tokyo 38 million

0   800   1600   2400   3200 km

Scale : One centimetre on this map is the same as 800 kilometres on the ground.

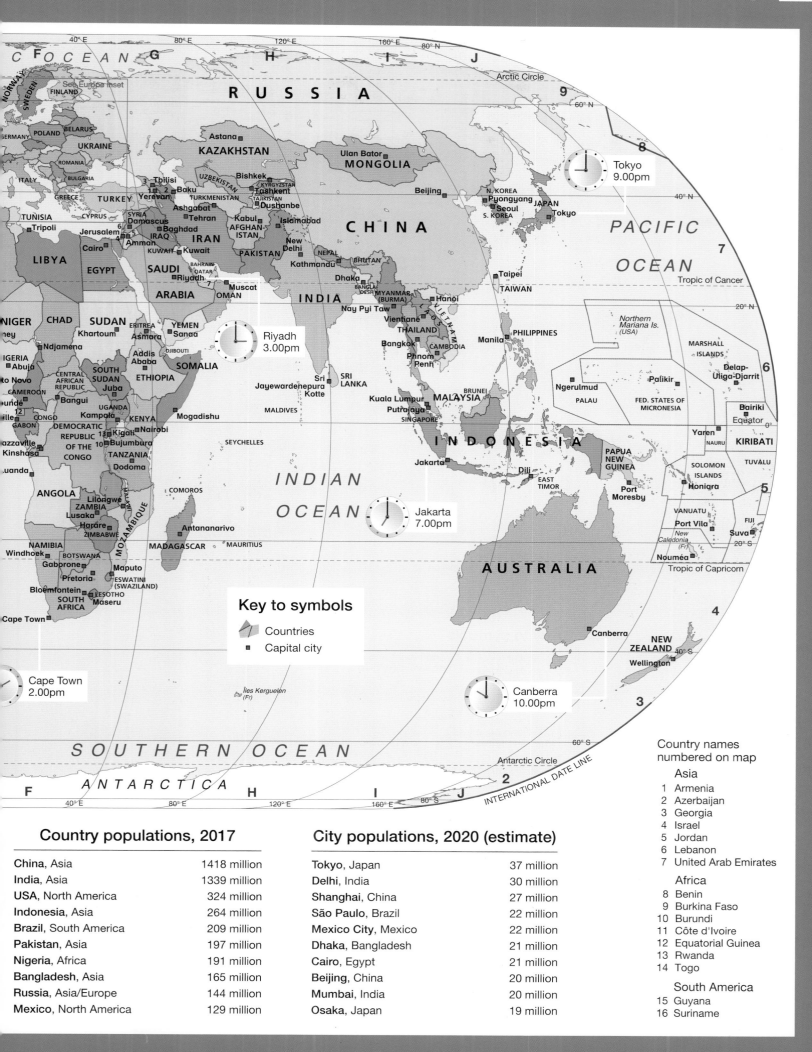

See Europa inset

Tokyo 9.00pm

Riyadh 3.00pm

Jakarta 7.00pm

Cape Town 2.00pm

Canberra 10.00pm

Key to symbols

Countries

Capital city

Country names numbered on map

Asia
1 Armenia
2 Azerbaijan
3 Georgia
4 Israel
5 Jordan
6 Lebanon
7 United Arab Emirates

Africa
8 Benin
9 Burkina Faso
10 Burundi
11 Côte d'Ivoire
12 Equatorial Guinea
13 Rwanda
14 Togo

South America
15 Guyana
16 Suriname

Country populations, 2017

China, Asia	1418 million
India, Asia	1339 million
USA, North America	324 million
Indonesia, Asia	264 million
Brazil, South America	209 million
Pakistan, Asia	197 million
Nigeria, Africa	191 million
Bangladesh, Asia	165 million
Russia, Asia/Europe	144 million
Mexico, North America	129 million

City populations, 2020 (estimate)

Tokyo, Japan	37 million
Delhi, India	30 million
Shanghai, China	27 million
São Paulo, Brazil	22 million
Mexico City, Mexico	22 million
Dhaka, Bangladesh	21 million
Cairo, Egypt	21 million
Beijing, China	20 million
Mumbai, India	20 million
Osaka, Japan	19 million

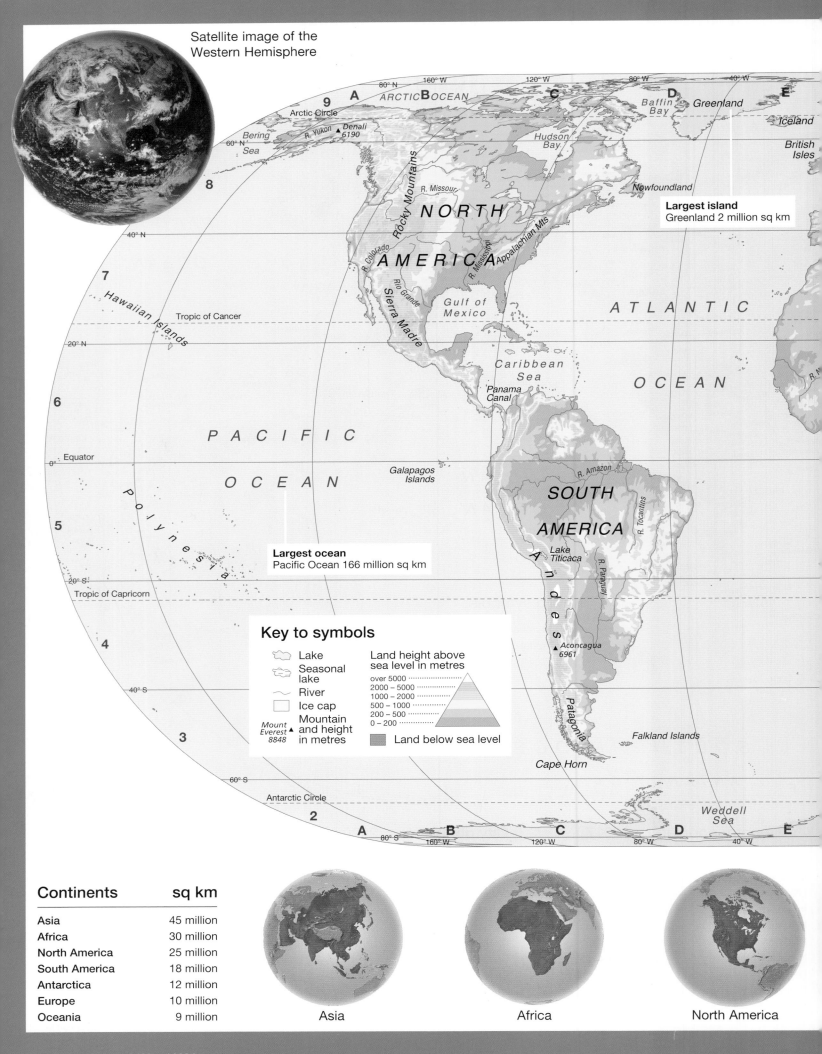

Satellite image of the
Western Hemisphere

80° N   160° W   120° W   80° W   40° W

9 **A** ARCTIC **B** OCEAN   **C**   **D**   **E**

Baffin
Bay   Greenland

Arctic Circle   Iceland

Bering   R. Yukon   ▲ Denali
8   Sea   6190   Hudson   British
60° N   Bay   Isles

R. Missouri   Newfoundland

N O R T H

Largest island
Greenland 2 million sq km

40° N
7   Hawaiian Islands   R. Colorado   Rocky Mountains   A M E R I C A   R. Mississippi   Appalachian Mts   A T L A N T I C

Tropic of Cancer   Rio Grande   Sierra Madre   Gulf of   R. M
20° N   Mexico   O C E A N

6   Caribbean
     Sea
Panama
Canal

P A C I F I C

Equator   0°
Galapagos
Islands   R. Amazon

O C E A N   SOUTH

5   P o l y n e s i a   AMERICA

Largest ocean
Pacific Ocean 166 million sq km

Lake
Titicaca   R. Tocantins

A n d e s   R. Paraguay

▲ Aconcagua
6961
20° S
Tropic of Capricorn

Key to symbols

🏞	Lake	**Land height above**
🏞	Seasonal lake	**sea level in metres**
〰	River	over 5000
▢	Ice cap	2000 – 5000
Mount Everest ▲ *8848*	Mountain and height in metres	1000 – 2000
		500 – 1000
		200 – 500
		0 – 200

Land below sea level

40° S   Patagonia

Falkland Islands

3   Cape Horn

60° S

Antarctic Circle   Weddell
Sea

2

A   **B**   **C**   **D**   **E**
80° S   160° W   120° W   80° W   40° W

Continents   sq km

Asia	45 million
Africa	30 million
North America	25 million
South America	18 million
Antarctica	12 million
Europe	10 million
Oceania	9 million

Asia   Africa   North America

0   800   1600   2400   3200 km

Scale : One centimetre on this map is the same as 800 kilometres on the ground.

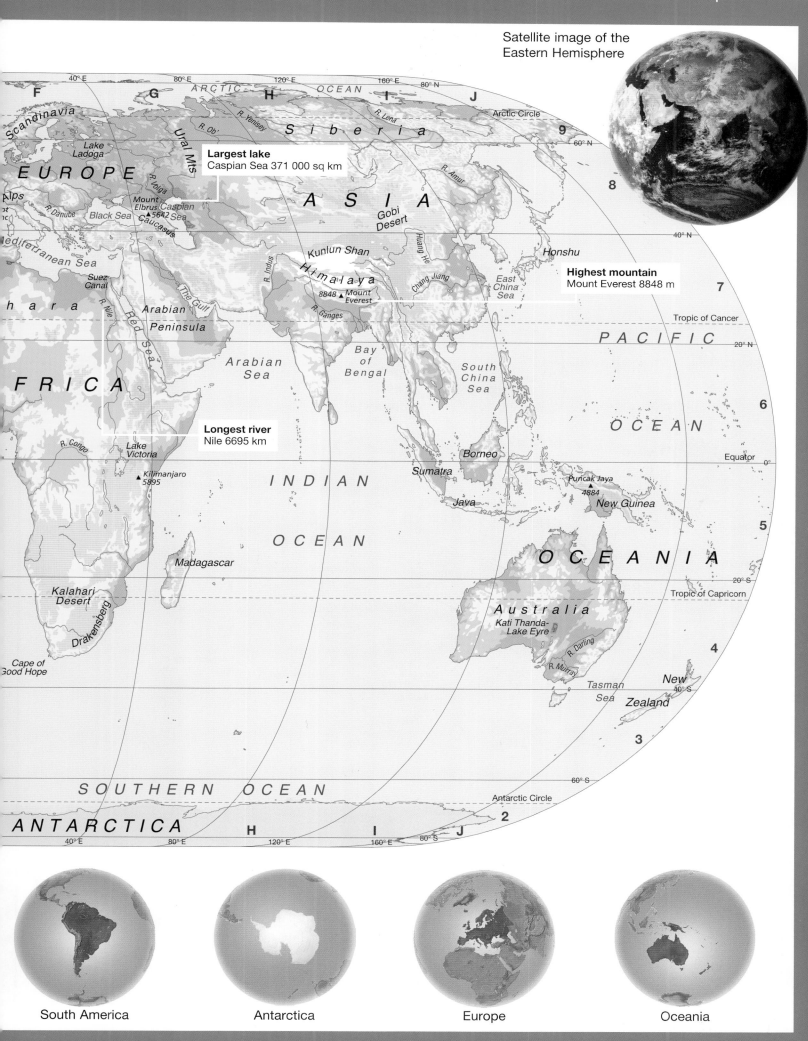

Satellite image of the
Eastern Hemisphere

Largest lake
Caspian Sea 371 000 sq km

Highest mountain
Mount Everest 8848 m

Longest river
Nile 6695 km

ARCTIC OCEAN

Scandinavia

Lake
Ladoga

EUROPE

R. Yenisey

R. Ob'

Ural Mts

R. Volga

R. Lena

Siberia

R. Amur

Arctic Circle

ASIA

Gobi
Desert

Alps

R. Danube

Black Sea

Mount
Elbrus Caspian
▲5642 Sea
Caucasus

Mediterranean Sea

Suez
Canal

hara

The Gulf

R. Nile

Arabian
Peninsula

Red Sea

R. Indus

Kunlun Shan

Himalaya

8848 ▲Mount
Everest

R. Ganges

Huang He

Chang Jiang

Honshu

East
China
Sea

FRICA

Arabian
Sea

Bay
of
Bengal

South
China
Sea

PACIFIC

Tropic of Cancer

OCEAN

Lake
Victoria

Kilimanjaro
▲ 5895

INDIAN

Sumatra

Borneo

Java

OCEAN

Puncak Jaya ▲
4884

New Guinea

Equator

Madagascar

Kalahari
Desert

Drakensberg

Cape of
Good Hope

OCEANIA

Australia

Kati Thanda-
Lake Eyre

R. Darling

R. Murray

Tropic of Capricorn

New
Zealand

Tasman
Sea

SOUTHERN OCEAN

Antarctic Circle

ANTARCTICA

South America

Antarctica

Europe

Oceania

Total population of Europe
(excluding Russia)
598 million

Country with most people
(excluding Russia)
Germany 82 million

Largest city
(Western Europe)
Paris 11 million

Largest country
(excluding Russia)
Ukraine 603 700 sq km

Largest city
Istanbul 15 million

Russia
Area 17 million sq km
Population 144 million

Key to symbols

Countries
Capital city
Important city/town

1 BELGIUM
2 BOSNIA AND HERZEGOVINA
3 KOSOVO
4 LIECHTENSTEIN
5 LUXEMBOURG
6 MONTENEGRO
7 NETHERLANDS
8 SLOVENIA
9 SWITZERLAND
10 VATICAN CITY

ARCTIC OCEAN

N W E S

Spitsbergen

Novaya Zemlya

White Sea

Jan Mayen (Norway)

ATLANTIC OCEAN

Faroe Islands (Denmark)

ICELAND
Reykjavík

RUSSIA

NORWAY
Oslo

SWEDEN
Stockholm

FINLAND
Helsinki

St Petersburg

Moscow

Gulf of Bothnia

Tallinn
ESTONIA
LATVIA
Riga

Baltic Sea

Edinburgh North Sea

DENMARK
Copenhagen

LITHUANIA
Vilnius
Minsk

RUSSIA

Belfast
Dublin
IRELAND

UNITED KINGDOM

BELARUS

Volgograd

Amsterdam
The Hague 7
London
Berlin
Warsaw

GERMANY
POLAND

Kiev

Brussels 1
English Channel
5
Prague

UKRAINE

Paris
Munich
CZECHIA
Vienna
SLOVAKIA
Bratislava

MOLDOVA
Chișinău

Odesa

FRANCE
Bern 9 4
AUSTRIA
Budapest
HUNGARY

Black Sea

Lyon
Ljubljana 8
Milan
SAN MARINO
MONACO
ANDORRA

Zagreb
CROATIA 2
Sarajevo
6 3
Skopje
ROMANIA
Belgrade
SERBIA
Bucharest

Caspian Sea

Bay of Biscay

Istanbul

PORTUGAL
Lisbon
Madrid
Barcelona
SPAIN
Balearic Islands
Corsica
10 ITALY
Rome
Tirana
ALBANIA
BULGARIA
Sofia
MACEDONIA
TURKEY

Adriatic Sea

Sardinia
GREECE
Aegean Sea

Gibraltar (UK)
Strait of Gibraltar

Sicily
MALTA
Crete
Athens
Rhodes

ASIA

Mediterranean Sea

AFRICA

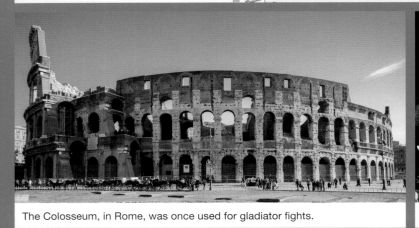

The Colosseum, in Rome, was once used for gladiator fights.

The Arc de Triomphe in France's capital city, Paris.

0 250 500 750 1000 1250 km
Scale : One centimetre on this map is the same as 250 kilometres on the ground.

Key to symbols

- Lake
- Seasonal lake
- River
- Ice cap
- Mountain and height in metres — Mount Elbrus ▲ 5642

Land height above sea level in metres
- over 5000
- 2000 – 5000
- 1000 – 2000
- 500 – 1000
- 200 – 500
- 0 – 200

Land below sea level

Total area of Europe
10 million sq km

Largest island
Great Britain 218 476 sq km

Longest river
Volga 3688 km

Highest mountain
Mount Elbrus 5642 m

Largest lake
Caspian Sea 371 000 sq km

Mount Etna, on the island of Sicily, is one of the world's most active volcanoes.

Narrow, steep sided inlets called fjords are found along the Norwegian coastline.

Scale : One centimetre on this map is the same as 250 kilometres on the ground.

0   250   500   750   1000   1250 km

The headquarters of the EU in Brussels.

The European Union (EU) was created in 1957 by the Treaty of Rome. The original members of the then European Economic Community (EEC) were Belgium, France, West Germany, Italy, Luxembourg and the Netherlands. Since then the EU has grown and now has 28 member states. The total population of the EU is now over half a billion. In 2016 the United Kingdom voted to leave the EU.

European Union

EU member
EU candidate
Non EU member

B.H.	BOSNIA AND HERZEGOVINA
KOS.	KOSOVO
L.	LIECHTENSTEIN
LUX.	LUXEMBOURG
MAC.	MACEDONIA
MOL.	MOLDOVA
MON.	MONTENEGRO
R.	RUSSIA
SL.	SLOVENIA
SWITZ.	SWITZERLAND

ICELAND
NORWAY
SWEDEN
FINLAND
ESTONIA
LATVIA
LITHUANIA
R.
DENMARK
UNITED KINGDOM
IRELAND
BELARUS
NETHERLANDS
GERMANY
POLAND
BELGIUM
LUX.
CZECHIA
UKRAINE
SLOVAKIA
SWITZ. L. AUSTRIA
HUNGARY
MOL.
FRANCE
SL.
CROATIA
ROMANIA
B.H.
SERBIA
ANDORRA
MON.
KOS.
BULGARIA
ITALY
ALBANIA MAC.
PORTUGAL
SPAIN
TURKEY
GREECE
MALTA
CYPRUS

Austria
Belgium
Bulgaria
Croatia
Cyprus
Czechia
Denmark
Estonia
Finland
France
Germany
Greece
Hungary
Ireland
Italy
Latvia
Lithuania
Luxembourg
Malta
Netherlands
Poland
Portugal
Romania
Slovakia
Slovenia
Spain
Sweden
United Kingdom

Key to symbols

- Countries
- ■ Capital city
- ○ Important city/town

N
W E
S

Shetland Islands

Orkney Islands

ATLANTIC OCEAN

Outer Hebrides

Inverness

Aberdeen

Fort William

SCOTLAND

Dundee

North Sea

Glasgow ○ ■ **Edinburgh**

Londonderry (Derry)

NORTHERN IRELAND ■ **Belfast**

Newcastle upon Tyne

UNITED

Middlesbrough

Isle of Man

Dundalk

York

IRELAND

Blackpool Bradford Leeds

Preston

Galway ■ **Dublin**

Irish Sea

Manchester

Liverpool Sheffield

KINGDOM

Stoke-on-Trent Derby Nottingham

Limerick

ENGLAND Norwich

Wolverhampton Leicester

Waterford

Birmingham

WALES Coventry

Cambridge

Ipswich

Cork

Oxford

Swansea **London** ■

Southend-on-Sea

Celtic Sea

Cardiff ■ Bristol Reading

BELGIUM

Southampton Brighton

Portsmouth

Bournemouth

Plymouth Torquay

English Channel

Channel Islands

FRANCE

Tower Bridge crosses the River Thames in London.

50 100 150 200 250 km

Scale : One centimetre on this map is the same as 50 kilometres on the ground.

Area recorded by satellite

Satellite

Direction of Earth's rotation

Orbit of satellite around Earth

Earth

Satellite images are recorded by sensors similar to television cameras which are carried aboard satellites. These satellites orbit 500 km above the Earth and images are beamed back to Earth.

Snow covered mountains in Scotland.

Mountains covered with heather and poor grass.

Much of the land in the UK is used for agriculture. This is why so much of the image shows greens and browns.

The image above is a simulated natural colour image of Great Britain and Ireland. The image was made on a clear, cloudless day so a lot of detail is visible. Notice the Shetland Islands in the far north, and the Orkney Islands south of them closer to the coast. The island of Skye off the west coast of Scotland also stands out clearly.

One of Scotland's famous glens, Glen Coe.

Total area of the United Kingdom
243 609 sq km

Largest lake
Lough Neagh 396 sq km

Highest mountain
Ben Nevis 1345 m

Largest island
Great Britain 218 476 sq km

Longest river
River Severn 354 km

Key to symbols

⌇ Lake

〜 River

Ben Nevis ▲
1345 Mountain and
       height in metres

Land height above
sea level in metres

over 1000
500 – 1000
200 – 500
100 – 200
0 – 100

Land below sea level

Map labels

N W E S

Shetland Islands
Mainland
Sumburgh Head

Orkney Islands
Mainland
Hoy
Pentland Firth
Duncansby Head

Cape Wrath

Outer Hebrides
Isle of Lewis
St Kilda
Harris
North Uist
Skye
South Uist
Rum
Coll
Tiree
Mull
Ben More 966
Jura
Islay
Arran
Inner Hebrides

The Minch

North West Highlands
Moray Firth
R. Spey
Loch Ness
Cairngorm Mts
Ben Macdui 1309
R. Dee
Ben Nevis 1345
Grampian Mts
Glen Coe
Loch Tay
R. Tay
Loch Lomond
Ochil Hills
R. Forth
Firth of Forth
R. Clyde
Firth of Clyde

Southern Uplands
Merrick 843
Cheviot Hills
R. Tweed
R. Tyne

North Channel
Antrim Hills
R. Bann
R. Foyle
Lough Neagh
Lower Lough Erne
Upper Lough Erne
Mourne Mts
Slieve Donard 852
Dundalk Bay

Malin Head
Donegal Bay
Achill I.
Lough Mask
Lough Corrib
Galway Bay
Lough Ree
R. Shannon
R. Boyne

Ireland
Lough Derg
Lugnaquilla Mtn 926
Wicklow Mts
R. Barrow
R. Shannon
R. Suir
Carrantuohill 1041
R. Blackwater
Cape Clear

Isle of Man
Solway Firth
Scafell Pike 978
Lake District
North York Moors
Flamborough Head
R. Tees
R. Ouse
Spurn Head

Great Britain
Pennines
High Peak
Kinder Scout 636
R. Mersey
Anglesey
Snowdon 1085
R. Dee
Cambrian Mountains
Cardigan Bay
R. Wye
Black Mountains 886
Brecon Beacons
R. Severn
R. Severn
R. Trent
The Wash
Norfolk Broads
The Fens
R. Great Ouse
R. Avon
Cotswold
Chiltern Hills
R. Thames
R. Thames
North Downs
South Downs
Beachy Head
Mendip Hills
Exmoor
Bristol Channel
Dartmoor
Yes Tor 619
R. Tamar
Bodmin Moor
Lyme Bay
Isle of Wight
Land's End
Start Point
Isles of Scilly

St George's Channel
St David's Head
Celtic Sea
English Channel
Channel Islands

Irish Sea

ATLANTIC OCEAN

North Sea

The South Downs drop down to the sea in chalk cliffs at Beachy Head.

50 100 150 200 250 km

Scale : One centimetre on this map is the same as 50 kilometres on the ground.

F
E
D
C
B
A

5
4
3

2°E
56° N
54° N
0°
2°W
4°W
6°W
56° N
54° N

N
E
S
W

North Sea

Irish Sea

North Channel

SCOTLAND

ENGLAND

NORTHERN IRELAND

IRELAND

Norfolk Broads

Cromer

King's Lynn
The Wash
R. Nene
R. Welland
Boston
Grantham
Loughborough
Nottingham
Louth
Skegness
Lincoln
R. Witham
Grimsby
Cleethorpes
Scunthorpe
R. Trent
Mansfield
Chesterfield
Derby
Stoke-on-Trent
Stafford
Kingston upon Hull
Spurn Head
R. Humber
Beverley
Goole
R. Ouse
Selby
Doncaster
Rotherham
Barnsley
Sheffield
Huddersfield
High Peak
Macclesfield
Oswestry
Flamborough Head
Bridlington
Scarborough
Whitby
North York Moors
R. Derwent
York
Harrogate
Ripon
R. Ure
Northallerton
R. Swale
R. Nidd
Leeds
Bradford
Halifax
Skipton
Rochdale
Oldham
Manchester
Stockport
Crewe
Chester
Wrexham
Mold
R. Clwyd
Rhyl
Colwyn Bay
Bala Lake
R. Dee
Festiniog
Pwllheli
Llŷn Peninsula
Snowdon 1085
Caernarfon
Caernarfon Bay
Bangor
Anglesey
Holyhead

Wicklow
Wicklow Head
Bray
Dún Laoghaire
Skerries

Hartlepool
Middlesbrough
Stockton-on-Tees
Darlington
R. Tees
Bishop Auckland
Durham
Sunderland
South Shields
Newcastle upon Tyne
R. Tyne
R. Wear
Morpeth
Alnwick
Berwick-upon-Tweed
Cheviot Hills
Coldstream
R. Tweed
Jedburgh
Hawick
R. Teviot
Galashiels
Peebles
Southern Uplands
Moffat
Lockerbie
Longtown
Carlisle
Penrith
Lake District
Scafell Pike 978
Windermere
Kendal
Pennines
R. Ribble
Burnley
Blackburn
Bolton
Bury
R. Mersey
Warrington
Ellesmere Port
Birkenhead
Liverpool
St Helens
Wigan
Preston
Southport
Formby
Blackpool
Morecambe Bay
Morecambe
Lancaster
Barrow-in-Furness
Whitehaven
Workington
Solway Firth

Isle of Man
(British Crown Dependency)
Douglas

Dumfries
Castle Douglas
Newton Stewart
Merrick 843
Whithorn
Stranraer
Girvan
Ayr
Prestwick
Irvine
Kilmarnock
East Kilbride
Paisley
Greenock
Dumbarton
Clydebank
Glasgow
Hamilton
Motherwell
R. Clyde
Firth of Clyde
Arran
Bute
Rothesay
Campbeltown
Mull of Kintyre
Port Ellen
Islay
Port Askaig
Jura
Colonsay
Mull
Firth of Lorn
Oban
Lochgilphead
Inveraray
Crianlarich
Ben More 1174
Loch Lomond
Loch Tay
Perth
Firth of Tay
Dundee
St Andrews
Glenrothes
Kirkcaldy
Dunfermline
Firth of Forth
Edinburgh
Livingston
Falkirk
Stirling
Ochil Hills
R. Forth

Larne
Newtownabbey
Bangor
Belfast
Lisburn
Antrim
Antrim Hills
Newcastle
Downpatrick
R. Lagan
Mourne Mts 852
Slieve Donard

0   20   40   60   80   100 km

Scale : One centimetre on this map is the same as 20 kilometres on the ground.

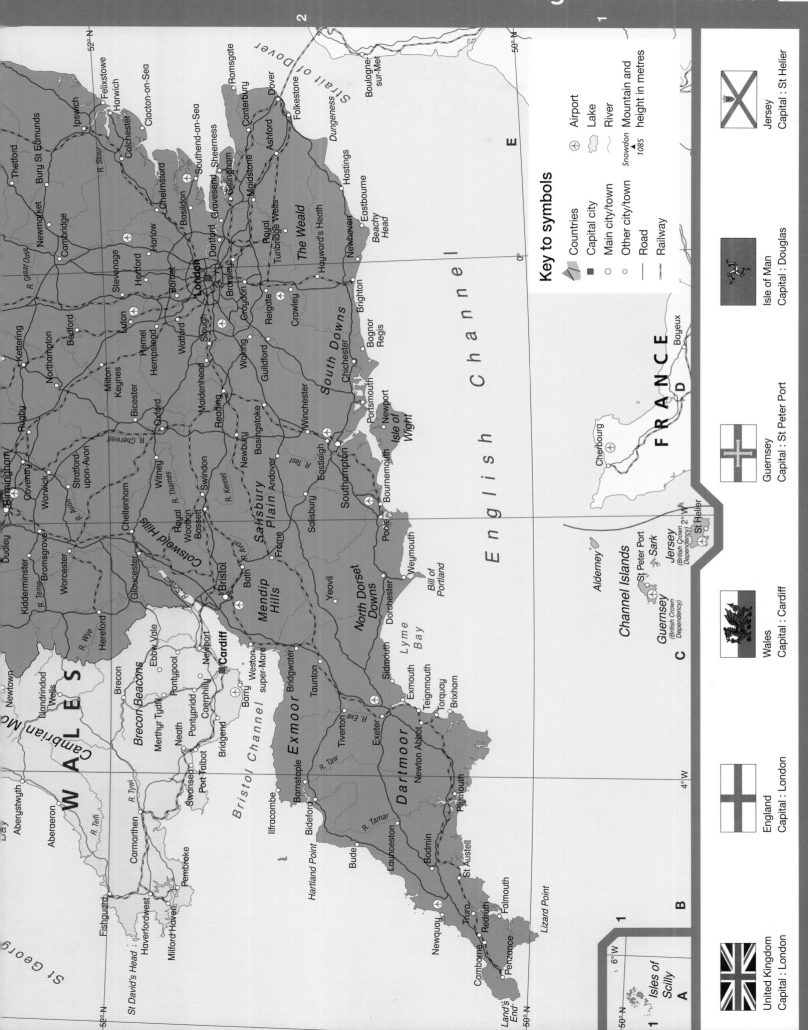

Key to symbols

Countries
Capital city
Main city/town
Other city/town
Road
Railway
Airport
Lake
River
Snowdon ▲ Mountain and
1085 height in metres

United Kingdom
Capital : London

England
Capital : London

Wales
Capital : Cardiff

Guernsey
Capital : St Peter Port

Isle of Man
Capital : Douglas

Jersey
Capital : St Helier

WALES

Cambrian Mo...
Newtown
Llandrindod Wells
Brecon Beacons
Brecon
Aberystwyth
Aberaeron
Fishguard
St David's Head
Haverfordwest
Milford Haven
Pembroke
Carmarthen
Merthyr Tydfil
Ebbw Vale
Pontypool
Neath
Pontypridd
Caerphilly
Swansea
Port Talbot
Bridgend
Barry
Newport
Cardiff
R. Tywi
R. Teifi
St George... Bay
R. Wye

Dudley
Kidderminster
Bromsgrove
Worcester
Hereford
Birmingham
Coventry
Warwick
Stratford-upon-Avon
Gloucester
Cheltenham
Cotswold Hills
Royal Wootton Bassett
Swindon
Rugby
Northampton
Kettering
Bedford
Milton Keynes
Bicester
Oxford
Witney
R. Cherwell
R. Avon
R. Teme
R. Severn

Thetford
Bury St Edmunds
Newmarket
Cambridge
Felixstowe
Harwich
Ipswich
Colchester
Clacton-on-Sea
Southend-on-Sea
R. Stour
R. Great Ouse

Stevenage
Hertford
Luton
Hemel Hempstead
Watford
Barnet
Harlow
Chelmsford
Basildon
London
Slough
Maidenhead
Reading
Newbury
Basingstoke
Andover
R. Thames
R. Kennet

Dartford
Gravesend
Sheerness
Gillingham
Maidstone
Royal Tunbridge Wells
Hayward's Heath
Ramsgate
Canterbury
Dover
Folkestone
Ashford
Hastings
Eastbourne
Beachy Head
Strait of Dover
Dungeness
The Weald
Newhaven
Brighton
Crawley
Reigate
Croydon
Bromley
Woking
Guildford
Chichester
Bognor Regis
South Downs

Winchester
Eastleigh
Southampton
Portsmouth
Newport
Isle of Wight
R. Test
Salisbury
Salisbury Plain
Frome
Yeovil
Bournemouth
Poole
Weymouth
Bill of Portland
North Dorset Downs
Dorchester
Lyme Bay
Sidmouth
Exmouth
Teignmouth
Torquay
Brixham
R. Exe
Mendip Hills
Bath
Bristol
Weston-super-Mare
Bridgwater
Taunton
Tiverton
Exeter
Exmoor
Barnstaple
Bideford
Ilfracombe
Hartland Point
R. Taw
R. Tamar
Dartmoor
Newton Abbot
Plymouth
Launceston
Bude
Bodmin
St Austell
Newquay
Truro
Redruth
Camborne
Penzance
Land's End
Lizard Point
Falmouth

Bristol Channel

English Channel

FRANCE
Boulogne-sur-Mer
Bayeux
Cherbourg

Channel Islands
Alderney
Guernsey (British Crown Dependency)
St Peter Port
Sark
Jersey (British Crown Dependency)
St Helier

Isles of Scilly

52°N
50°N
0°
2°W
4°W
6°W

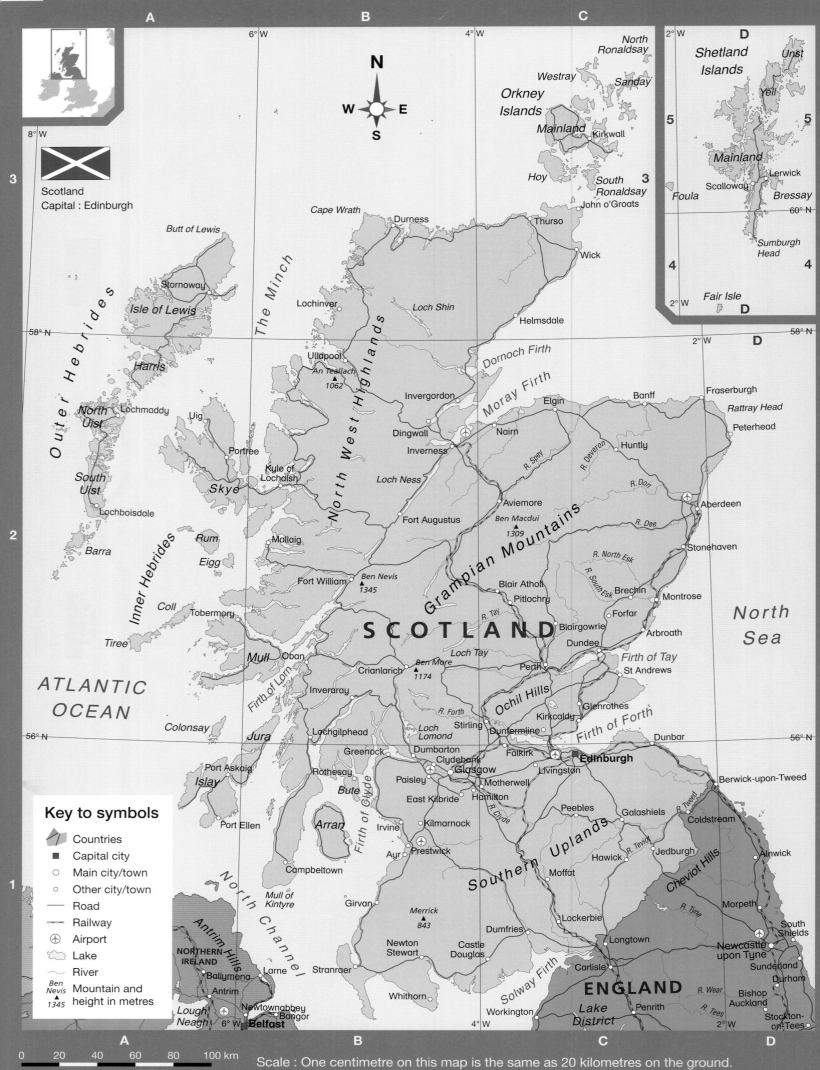

Scotland
Capital : Edinburgh

Key to symbols

◤ Countries
■ Capital city
◉ Main city/town
○ Other city/town
— Road
╫ Railway
✈ Airport
〰 Lake
〰 River
▲ Ben Nevis 1345 Mountain and height in metres

Scale : One centimetre on this map is the same as 20 kilometres on the ground.

0 20 40 60 80 100 km

Key to symbols

- Countries
- ■ Capital city
- ○ Main city/town
- ○ Other city/town
- Road
- Railway
- ⊕ Airport
- Lake
- River
- *Carrantuohill* ▲ 1041 Mountain and height in metres

N W E S

SCOTLAND

Port Askaig *Jura* 6° W Rothesay *Bute* Irvine
Islay Prestwick
Port Ellen *Arran* Ayr
Campbeltown Firth of Clyde
Mull of Kintyre Girvan
North Channel Stranraer

Malin Head

Bloody Foreland
Errigal ▲ 752
Letterkenny
Portrush Coleraine
Lough Foyle Antrim Hills
Londonderry (Derry) R. Bann Larne
Strabane Ballymena
Antrim
NORTHERN
Donegal Cookstown *Lough Neagh* Newtownabbey
Omagh **IRELAND** Bangor
Lower Lough Erne Dungannon Belfast ■
Donegal Bay R. Lagan Lisburn
Armagh Downpatrick
Sligo Enniskillen Monaghan Newry Newcastle
Erris Head *Upper Lough Erne* ▲ 852 Slieve Donard
Belmullet Mourne Mts
Isle of Man (British Crown Dependency)
Ballina *Lough Allen* Dundalk
54° N *Lough Conn* Carrick-on-Shannon Cavan *Dundalk Bay* 54° N
Achill Island Charlestown Drogheda
Castlebar
Westport Longford *Lough Ree* Navan *Irish Sea*
Lough Mask Claremorris Roscommon Skerries
Connemara *Lough Corrib* R. Suck Mullingar R. Boyne
Galway Athlone **Dublin** ■
Galway Bay **IRELAND** R. Liffey Dún Laoghaire
Aran Islands Tullamore Naas Bray
Lough Derg Portlaoise R. Barrow Wicklow Mts Wicklow
Wicklow Head
Ennis Roscrea R. Nore
ATLANTIC OCEAN Nenagh Carlow Arklow
Kilkee R. Shannon Thurles Kilkenny
Kilrush Limerick R. Suir Enniscorthy
Tipperary Carrick-on-Suir New Ross Wexford
Cahir Clonmel Rosslare
Tralee *Knockmealdown Mts* Waterford St George's Channel
Dingle Mallow R. Blackwater Fermoy Dungarvan Fishguard
Dingle Bay *Carrantuohill* ▲ 1041 Youghal **WALES**
Killarney *Boggeragh Mts* St David's Head
52° N Sneem R. Lee Cork Haverfordwest
Cobh Milford Haven
Bantry Pembroke
Old Head of Kinsale
Skibbereen
Mizen Head *Cape Clear*

Celtic Sea

10° W 8° W 6° W

|Ireland
Capital : Dublin | Northern Ireland
Capital : Belfast |

Scale : One centimetre on this map is the same as 20 kilometres on the ground.

0 20 40 60 80 100 km

A B C D E F G H I J

25°W 20°W 15°W 10°W 5°W 0° 5°E 10°E 15°E 20°E

6

N
W E
S

Arctic Circle

65°N

Akureyri

ICELAND

Reykjavik Vatnajökull

Seydisfjördur

Surtsey

Tromsø

Lofoten Islands

Narvik

Bodø

Gällivare

5

Norwegian Sea

N O R W A Y

Trondheim

Östersund

Sundsvall

60°N

Ålesund

Galdhøpiggen 2469
Lillehammer

Bergen

Umeå

S W E D E N

Uppsala

Drammen

Oslo

Västerås

Key to symbols

Countries
Capital city
○ Main city/town
○ Other city/town
— Road
Railway
Canal
⊕ Airport
Lake
River

Galdhøpiggen
▲ Mountain and
2469 height in metres

Faroe Islands (Denmark)

Shetland Islands

Orkney Islands

Inverness

Ben Nevis 1344
Grampian Mountains

Glasgow

Aberdeen

Outer Hebrides

Stavanger

Karlstad

Örebro

Stockh

Norrköping

Vänern

Vättern

Jönköping

Gotland

Kristiansand

Gothenburg

Skagerrak

Aalborg

Kattegat

Halmstad

Öland

Karlskrona

ATLANTIC OCEAN

55°N

Londonderry (Derry)

Belfast

Carlisle

Newcastle upon Tyne

Dundee

Edinburgh

North Sea

DENMARK

Aarhus

Copenhagen

Malmö

Bornholm

Baltic

3

Galway

IRELAND

Limerick

Dublin

Blackpool
Liverpool

Irish Sea

Leeds

Manchester

Sheffield

U N I T E D K I N G D O M

Esbjerg

Odense

Kiel

Gdańsk

Koszalin

Cork

Wexford

Birmingham

Nottingham

Hamburg

Rostock

Szczecin

Bydgoszcz

Swansea

Norwich

Groningen

Bremen

R.Elbe

50°N

Cardiff

Oxford

R.Thames

Bristol

London

Southampton

Plymouth

Dover
Strait of Dover

NETHERLANDS

Amsterdam
The Hague

Rotterdam

Bruges

Calais

IJsselmeer

Eindhoven

Antwerp

Duisburg

R.Weser

Bielefeld

Dortmund

Essen

Düsseldorf

Hannover

Magdeburg

R.Elbe

Berlin

Poznań

Zielona Góra

R.Oder

P O L A

English Channel

Channel Islands

Brest

Le Havre

Amiens

Rouen

Lille

BELGIUM

Brussels

Liège

Cologne

Bonn

GERMANY

Leipzig

Dresden

Erfurt

Wrocław

Sudeten Mts.

Kato

2

LUXEMBOURG

Luxembourg

Mainz

Frankfurt

Prague

Plzeň

CZECHIA (CZECH REPUBLIC)

Ostrava

Brno

Rennes

Caen

R.Seine

Reims

Nancy

R.Rhine

Karlsruhe

Nuremberg

SLO

Nantes

Le Mans

Paris

Orléans

R.Seine

Strasbourg

Stuttgart

R.Danube

R.Inn

Linz

Vienna

Bratisla

La Rochelle

Tours

R.Loire

Poitiers

Dijon

F R A N C E

Basel

Bern

Zürich

SWITZERLAND

LIECHTENSTEIN

Munich

Salzburg

Innsbruck

AUSTRIA

Graz

Budapes

H U

45°N

5°W

0°

5°E

10°E

15°E

E F G H I J

0 100 200 300 400 500 km

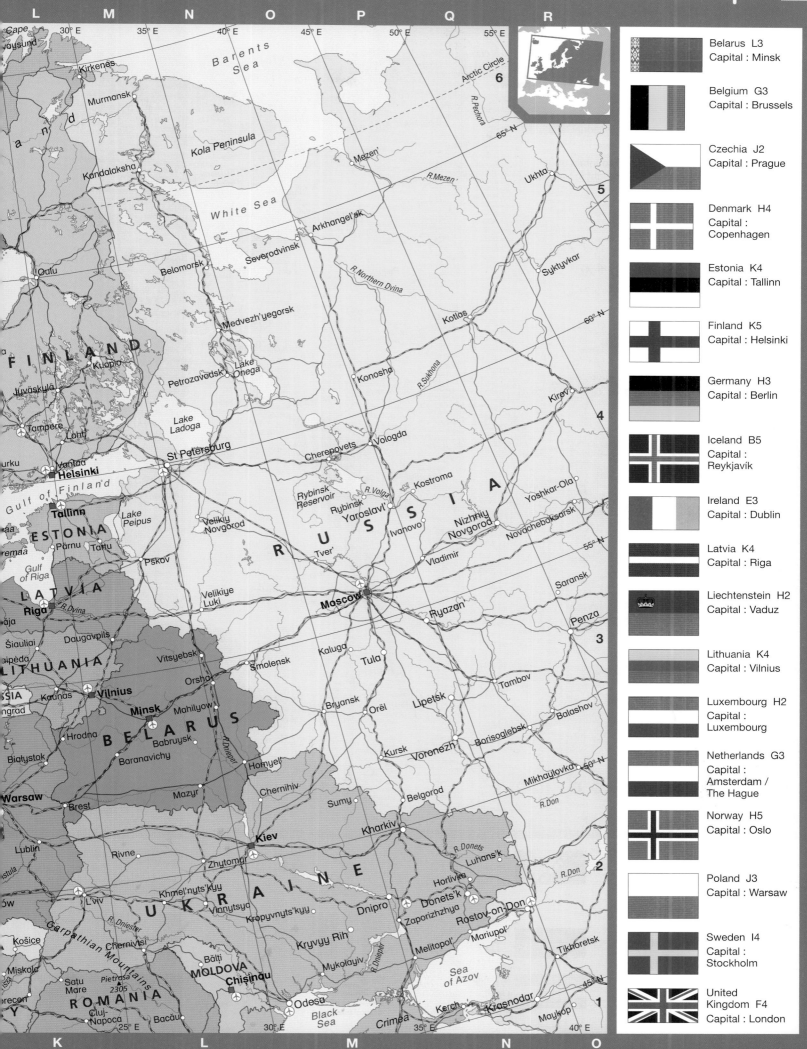

Belarus L3
Capital : Minsk

Belgium G3
Capital : Brussels

Czechia J2
Capital : Prague

Denmark H4
Capital : Copenhagen

Estonia K4
Capital : Tallinn

Finland K5
Capital : Helsinki

Germany H3
Capital : Berlin

Iceland B5
Capital : Reykjavík

Ireland E3
Capital : Dublin

Latvia K4
Capital : Riga

Liechtenstein H2
Capital : Vaduz

Lithuania K4
Capital : Vilnius

Luxembourg H2
Capital : Luxembourg

Netherlands G3
Capital : Amsterdam / The Hague

Norway H5
Capital : Oslo

Poland J3
Capital : Warsaw

Sweden I4
Capital : Stockholm

United Kingdom F4
Capital : London

A B C D E F G

Key to symbols

Countries		Canal	
Capital city		Airport	
Main city/town		Lake	
Other city/town		Seasonal lake	
Road		River	
Railway		Mont Blanc 4810 ▲	Mountain and height in metres

4

3

2

1

ATLANTIC OCEAN

5°W 10°E 5°E

UNITED KINGDOM
Swansea Cardiff Birmingham Oxford Norwich
Bristol R. Thames London
Southampton Dover Strait of Dover
Plymouth 50°N
English Channel Calais Lille
Channel Islands Le Havre Amiens Rouen R. Seine
Brest Caen
Rennes Le Mans Paris
Nantes R. Loire Orléans R. Loire
La Rochelle Poitiers Tours Dijon
Bay of Biscay Limoges Clermont-Ferrand Lyon
FRANCE
Massif Central
R. Rhône
Grenoble Mont Blanc 4810

NETHERLANDS Groningen Bremen
Amsterdam IJsselmeer Bielefeld Hannover Berl
The Hague Rotterdam Duisburg Dortmund Magde
BELGIUM Antwerp Essen Düsseldorf Cologne Leipzig
Brussels Liège Bonn R. Rhine Erfurt Drese
Bruges GERMAN
Luxembourg Mainz Frankfurt
LUXEMBOURG Nancy Nuremberg
Reims Strasbourg Karlsruhe R. Danube
Basel Stuttgart Munich R. I
Geneva Zürich Salz
SWITZERLAND LIECHTENSTEIN Innsbruck
Bern Turin A Bolzano S
Milan Bergamo L P
Piacenza Verona R. Po Veni
Genoa Bologna SAN MARINO Sar
Nice Florence Ma
Monte-Carlo Pisa I
MONACO Perugia T A
Côte d'Azur VATICAN CITY
Corsica Rome
Ajaccio L

45°N 10°W
40°N

Cape Finisterre A Coruña
Gijón Santander Bayonne
Vigo Cantabrian Mountains Bilbao
Braga León Burgos Pamplona
Oporto R. Douro R. Ebro Pyrenees
Coimbra Valladolid R. Duero Aneto 3404 ANDORRA
PORTUGAL Salamanca Zaragoza Andorra la Vella
Madrid Barcelona
SPAIN Costa Brava
Lisbon R. Tagus
Badajoz
Sierra Morena Albacete Valencia Balearic Sea
Córdoba Palma de Mallorca Minorca
Seville R. Guadalquivir Granada Alicante Ibiza Majorca
Cape St Vincent Cádiz Sierra Nevada Cartagena Balearic Islands
Faro Málaga Costa del Sol Almería
Tangier Gibraltar (UK) M
Ceuta (Spain)
Tétouan Melilla (Spain)
Rabat Fez Oran Sidi Bel Abbès Chlef Constantine e
Casablanca Meknès Oujda d
MOROCCO ALGERIA Sétif Annaba Bizerte
Batna Tunis
Marrakesh Béni Mellal Tébessa TUNISIA Sousse
Gafsa Sfax
Gulf of Gabès

Bordeaux R. Garonne
Toulouse Montpellier Avignon Marseille Perpignan
35°N

Sardinia Cagliari Tyrrhenian Sea

Mediterranean Sea Palermo

Gulf of Gascony

Algiers

C D E F G
5°W 0° 5°E 10°E

	Albania H3 Capital : Tirana		Bosnia and Herzegovina H3 Capital : Sarajevo		Cyprus K1 Capital : Nicosia		Hungary H4 Capital : Budapest
	Andorra E3 Capital : Andorra la Vella		Bulgaria I3 Capital : Sofia		France E4 Capital : Paris		Italy G3 Capital : Rome
	Austria G4 Capital : Vienna		Croatia H4 Capital : Zagreb		Greece I2 Capital : Athens		Macedonia I3 Capital : Skopje

Map of Southern Europe

H — I — J — K — L — M

20° E · 25° E · 30° E · 35° E · 40° E

POLAND
Szczecin · Bydgoszcz · Poznań · Zielona Góra · Wrocław · Łódź · Katowice · Kraków · Białystok · Warsaw · Lublin
R. Vistula · R. Oder · Sudeten Mts

BELARUS
Baranavichy · Mazyr · Brest · Homyel

Prague · CZECHIA (CZECH REPUBLIC) · Brno · Ostrava
Kursk · Sumy · Chernihiv · Belgorod

SLOVAKIA
Vienna · Bratislava · Miskolc · Košice
R. Tisza · Carpathian Mountains

Kiev · Rivne · Zhytomyr · Khmel'nyts'kyy · L'viv
UKRAINE · Vinnytsya · Kropyvnyts'kyy · Dnipro · Kharkiv · Horlivka · Donets'k · Luhans'k
R. Dnieper · R. Donets · R. Don

HUNGARY
Graz · Budapest · Debrecen · Szeged · Pécs
Satu Mare · Pietrosa 2305 · Cluj Napoca
Chernivtsi · Bălți · **MOLDOVA** · Chişinău
Kryvyy Rih · Mykolayiv · Zaporizhzhya · Melitopol' · Mariupol' · Odesa

RUSSIA
Rostov-on-Don · Tikhoretsk · Krasnodar · Maykop

SLOVENIA · Ljubljana · Zagreb · **CROATIA** · Rijeka
ROMANIA · Timişoara · Braşov · Galaţi · Transylvanian Alps · Bacău · Ploieşti
Sea of Azov · Kerch · Crimea · Sevastopol' · Crimea: Administered by Russia · Sochi · GEORGIA

Banja Luka · **BOSNIA AND HERZEGOVINA** · Sarajevo · Split · Dinaric Alps
R. Danube · Novi Sad · Belgrade · **SERBIA** · Craiova · **Bucharest** · R. Danube · Ruse · Constanţa

MONTENEGRO · Dubrovnik · Podgorica · Shkodër · Niš · Balkan Mts · Sofia · **BULGARIA** · Varna · Burgas
Black Sea · Zonguldak

Bari · Brindisi · Taranto · **ALBANIA** · Tirana · Pristina · KOSOVO · Skopje · **MACEDONIA** · Bitola · Plovdiv · Edirne
Istanbul · Samsun · Trabzon · Ordu

Mt Vesuvius 1281 · Mount Olympus 2911 · Corfu · Ioannina · Pindus Mts · **GREECE** · Larisa · Thessaloniki · R. Evros · Gallipoli · Çanakkale · Bursa · Eskişehir · **Ankara** · Çorum · Sivas
R. Kızılırmak · **TURKEY** · Kütahya

Catanzaro · Reggio di Calabria · Catania · Aegean Sea · Patras · Corinth · **Athens** · Kalamata
Izmir · Konya · Taurus Mountains · Kayseri · Malatya · Gaziantep · Adana

Ionian Sea · Rhodes · Denizli · Antalya · Alanya
Aleppo · Latakia · **SYRIA**

Valletta · MALTA · Crete · Iraklion · Nicosia · **CYPRUS** · Limassol · Hamāh · Homs · Tripoli
Beirut · **LEBANON** · **Damascus**

Mediterranean Sea · Haifa · Irbid · **ISRAEL** · Tel Aviv-Yafo · **Amman** · **Jerusalem**

20° E · 25° E · 30° E · 35° E

Flag	Country	Capital
	Malta G2	Capital : Valletta
	Portugal C2	Capital : Lisbon
	Slovakia H4	Capital : Bratislava
	Switzerland F4	Capital : Bern
	Moldova J4	Capital : Chişinău
	Romania I4	Capital : Bucharest
	Slovenia G4	Capital : Ljubljana
	Turkey J2	Capital : Ankara
	Montenegro H3	Capital : Podgorica
	Serbia I3	Capital : Belgrade
	Spain C3	Capital : Madrid
	Ukraine J4	Capital : Kiev

Largest country
Russia 17 million sq km

Country with most people
China 1418 million

Total population of Asia
(including Russia)
4648 million

Russia
Area 17 million sq km
Population 144 million

Largest city
Tokyo 37 million

ARCTIC OCEAN

N
W E
S

The British Isles
at the same scale.

EUROPE

St Petersburg

Moscow

Perm

RUSSIA

Yakutsk

Sea of
Okhotsk

Sakhalin

Chelyabinsk

Volgograd

Omsk

Novosibirsk

Irkutsk

Lake
Baikal

Sapporo

Black
Sea

Ankara

GEORGIA

TURKEY

Tbilisi

Yerevan

Baku

CYPRUS

LEBANON

SYRIA

ISRAEL

Damascus

Amman

JORDAN

Baghdad

IRAQ

KUWAIT

Kuwait

Riyadh

SAUDI
ARABIA

Sanaa

YEMEN

Aden

Socotra
(Yemen)

AFRICA

Red
Sea

Arabian
Sea

KAZAKHSTAN

Astana

Aral
Sea

Lake
Balkhash

UZBEKISTAN

TURKMENISTAN

Ashgabat

Tehran

IRAN

Tashkent

Almaty

Ürümqi

Bishkek

Dushanbe

Kabul

AFGHANISTAN

Islamabad

Lahore

PAKISTAN

Delhi

Karachi

BAHRAIN

QATAR

UNITED
ARAB
EMIRATES

Muscat

OMAN

New
Delhi

INDIA

Mumbai

Hyderabad

Chennai

Ulan
Bator

MONGOLIA

Harbin

Shenyang

Lanzhou

Xi'an

Beijing

Tianjin

CHINA

Chongqing

Wuhan

Nanjing

Shanghai

Guangzhou

Hong
Kong

NEPAL

Kathmandu

Thimphu

BHUTAN

BANGLADESH

Dhaka

Kolkata

Mandalay

Hanoi

MYANMAR
(BURMA)

Nay Pyi Taw

Yangon

Vientiane

LAOS

THAILAND

Bangkok

CAMBODIA

Phnom Penh

Ho Chi
Minh City

VIETNAM

Sea of
Japan
(East
Sea)

JAPAN

Tokyo

NORTH
KOREA

Pyongyang

Seoul

SOUTH
KOREA

Kobe

Osaka

Fukuoka

Taipei

TAIWAN

PACIFIC
OCEAN

South
China
Sea

Luzon

PHILIPPINES

Manila

Mindanao

Davao

Bay
of
Bengal

Andaman Is
(India)

SRI
LANKA

Sri Jayewardenepura Kotte

Colombo

MALDIVES

Nicobar Is
(India)

BRUNEI

MALAYSIA

Kuala Lumpur

Putrajaya

Singapore

SINGAPORE

Borneo

Celebes

Sumatra

INDONESIA

Makassar

Java

Jakarta

Surabaya

Dili

EAST
TIMOR

INDIAN OCEAN

Key to symbols

Countries

Capital city

Important city/town

1 ARMENIA
2 AZERBAIJAN
3 TAJIKISTAN
4 KYRGYZSTAN

Shanghai is China's largest city.

A fruit stall in the Chinatown market, Kuala Lumpur, Malaysia.

0 500 1000 1500 2000 2500 km

Scale : One centimetre on this map is the same as 500 kilometres on the ground.

Total area of Asia
45 million sq km

Largest lake
Caspian Sea 371 000 sq km

ARCTIC OCEAN

N
W E
S

EUROPE

Ural Mountains

R. Yenisey

R. Ob

West Siberian Plain

Central Siberian Plateau

R. Lena

Siberia

Sea of Okhotsk

Sakhalin

R. Angara

R. Lena

R. Amur

Black Sea

Caspian Lowland

R. Ob

R. Irtysh

R. Yenisey

Lake Baikal

R. Argun

Hokkaido

Caucasus

Caspian Sea

Aral Sea

Lake Balkhash

R. Selenga

Altai Mts

Gobi Desert

Sea of Japan (East Sea)

Honshu

R. Tigris

Elburz Mountains

Zagros Mountains

Ysyk-Köl

Tien Shan

Kyushu

R. Euphrates

The Gulf

Hindu Kush

K2 8611 ▲

Tarim Basin

Kunlun Shan

Huang He

East China Sea

Red Sea

Arabian Peninsula

Plateau of Tibet

Himalaya

Chang Jiang

Longest river
Chang Jiang 6380 km

Taiwan

PACIFIC OCEAN

R. Indus

Thar Desert

Annapurna 8091 ▲

▲ Mount Everest 8848

R. Ganges

R. Irrawaddy

Gulf of Aden

Arabian Sea

Deccan

Bay of Bengal

R. Mekong

Luzon

Philippines

AFRICA

South China Sea

Mindanao

Highest mountain
Mount Everest 8848 m

Sri Lanka

Key to symbols

Lake
Seasonal lake
River
Ice cap
Mountain Everest ▲ 8848 Mountain and height in metres

Land height above sea level in metres

over 5000
2000 – 5000
1000 – 2000
500 – 1000
200 – 500
0 – 200

Land below sea level

Largest island
Borneo 745 561 sq km

Borneo

Celebes

Sumatra

Java

INDIAN OCEAN

Rice is grown on terraced hillsides on the Indonesian island of Bali.

Mount Everest on the border between China and Nepal.

0   500   1000   1500   2000   2500 km

Scale : One centimetre on this map is the same as 500 kilometres on the ground.

3   4   5   6

60° N   70° N   80° N

10° W

A
B
C
D
E
F
G
H

Key to symbols

- Countries
- ■ Capital city
- ○ Main city/town
- ∘ Other city/town
- — Road
- —— Railway
- 〰 Canal
- ✈ Airport
- Lake
- ～ River
- *Mount Elbrus* ▲ 5642   Mountain and height in metres

UNITED KINGDOM

Birmingham
Manchester
Leeds
Liverpool
London
Edinburgh

Orkney Islands
Shetland Islands
Faroe Islands (Denmark)

Jan Mayen (Norway)

Arctic Circle

Norwegian Sea

North Sea

Svalbard (Norway)
Spitsbergen

Franz Josef Land

ARCTIC

Trondheim
Bergen
Drammen
Oslo
Gothenburg
Stockholm
Västerås
Uppsala

NORWAY
SWEDEN
FINLAND

Baltic Sea

Gulf of Bothnia

Umeå
Turku
Tampere
Helsinki
Tallinn

Lapland

North Cape
Tromsø
Murmansk
Kola Peninsula
Kandalaksha

Barents Sea

Novaya Zemlya

Kara Sea

White Sea
Lake Onega
Lake Ladoga
Petrozavodsk
Arkhangel'sk
Mezen'

Gyda Peninsula

ESTONIA
LATVIA
LITHUANIA
Riga
Vilnius
BELARUS
Minsk

St. Petersburg
Velikiy Novgorod
Velikiye Luki
Tver'
Smolensk
Moscow
Yaroslavl'
Vologda

R. Northern Dvina
Kotlas
Syktyvkar
Ukhta

R. Pechora
Mt Narodhnaya 1895
R. Pechora

Vorkuta

Salekhard

Nadym

Urengoy

SLOVAKIA
HUNGARY
Budapest
ROMANIA
Chişinău
MOLDOVA
Bucharest
Galaţi

POLAND
Carpathian Mountains
L'viv
Zhytomyr
R. Dniester
R. Dnieper
Kyiv
UKRAINE
Bryansk
Tula
Orël
Ryazan'
Nizhniy Novgorod
Ivanovo
R. Volga
Kirov
Perm'
R. Kama
Izhevsk
Yekaterinburg

Ural Mountains

RUSSIA

West Siberian Plain

Surgut
Nizhnevartovsk
R. Ob'
Tomsk

Odesa
Kryvyy Rih
Dnipro
Kharkiv
Donetsk
R. Donets
R. Don
Voronezh
Tambov
Penza
Ul'yanovsk
Saransk
Kazan'
Naberezhnyye Chelny
Ufa
Tol'yatti
Samara
Magnitogorsk
Chelyabinsk
Kurgan
Tyumen'
R. Irtysh
R. Irtysh

Sevastopol
Crimea: Administered by Russia
Black Sea
Zonguldak
Samsun
Sivas
Sochi
Krasnodar
Rostov-on-Don
R. Don
Volgograd
R. Volga
Saratov
R. Ural
Ural'sk
Orenburg
Aktobe
R. Tobol
Kostanay
R. Ishim
Petropavlovsk
Omsk
Novosibirsk
Kemerovo
Novokuznetsk

Caspian Lowland
Astrakhan'
Atyrau
Fort Shevchenko
Aktau
Makhachkala
Grozny
Caspian Sea
Beyneu
Ustyurt Plateau
Aral Sea
Aral'sk
Zhezkazgan
Karagandy
Astana
Pavlodar
Barnaul
Biysk
Rubtsovsk
Ust'-Kamenogorsk
Semey

TURKEY
Kayseri
Malatya
Gaziantep
Erzurum
Bat'umi
GEORGIA
Tbilisi
Mount Elbrus 5642
Caucasus
ARMENIA
Yerevan
Mt Ararat 5165
AZERBAIJAN
Gäncä
Baku

KAZAKHSTAN
Kyzylorda
Aktogay
Balkhash
Lake Balkhash
Lake Zaysan
Karamay

SYRIA
IRAQ
Mosul
Erbil
Baghdad
Dayr az Zawr
R. Euphrates
R. Tigris
Basra
Kermanshah
Hamadan
Ahvaz
Isfahan
Qom
IRAN
Tehran
Tabriz
Rasht
Karaj
Qazvin
Gorgan
Sabzevar
TURKMENISTAN
Türkmenbaşy
Türkmenabat
Ashgabat
UZBEKISTAN
Urganch
R. Amu Darya
Buxoro
Shymkent
Tashkent
R. Syr Darya
KYRGYZSTAN
Bishkek
Almaty
Yining
CHINA
Lake Van
Lake Zaysan
Ürümqi

20° E   30° E   40° E   50° E   60° E   70° E   80° E
50° N   40° N   30° N

F   G   H   I   J

2
1

0   200   400   600   800 km

Scale : One centimetre on this map is the same as 200 kilometres on the ground.

Map of Russia

ARCTIC OCEAN

90° N

80° N

70° N

60° N

160° W

170° W

180°

170° E

160° E

U.S.A.

Arctic Circle

Nome

Norton Sound

Bering Strait

Chukchi Sea

Wrangel Island

Bering Sea

East Siberian Sea

Ambarchik

Anadyr

Gizhiga

Kolyma Range

R. Kolyma

New Siberian Islands

Laptev Sea

Kozach'ye

R. Indigirka

Severnaya Zemlya

Taymyr Peninsula

Nordvik

Ust'-Olenek

R. Olenek

Khatanga

R. Kotuy

Verkhoyansk

Cherskogo Range

Omsukchan

Kamchatka

Ust-Kamchatsk

Magadan

R. Lena

Verkhoyansk Range

El'ginskiy

R. Indigirka

Peninsula

Noril'sk

Olenek

Allakh-Yun'

Okhotsk

Petropavlovsk-Kamchatskiy

R. Kotuy

R. Lower Tunguska

S i b e r i a

R. Olenek

R. Vilyuy

R. Aldan

Sea of Okhotsk

Ozernovskiy

50° N

R U S S I A

Central

Tura

Verkhneviluysk

Yakutsk

Ayan

Okha

Siberian

R. Lena

Lensk

Aldan

R. Uchur

Sakhalin

Kuril Islands

R. Stony Tunguska

Plateau

R. Lena

Stanovoy Range

R. Amur

Aleksandrovsk-Sakhalinskiy

Poronaysk

150° E

R. Yenisey

R. Angara

Ust'-Ilimsk

Tynda

Svobodnyy

Komsomol'sk-na-Amure

Yuzhno-Sakhalinsk

Kuril'sk

Administered by Russia, claimed by Japan

Ust'-Kut

Skovorodino

R. Amur

Khabarovsk

Korsakov

Wakkanai

Kansk

Bratsk

R. Lena

Blagoveshchensk

Sikhote-Alin'

Kushiro

Krasnoyarsk

Lake Baikal

Sretensk

Yichun

R. Amur

Jiamusi

Hokkaido

Sapporo

JAPAN

Abakan

Usol'ye-Sibirskoye

Chita

Karymskoye

C H I N A

Jixi

Hakodate

Hachinohe

Irkutsk

Borzya

Fuyu

Daqing

Vladivostok

Nakhodka

Aomori

Kyzyl

Ulan-Ude

Manzhouli

Qiqihar

Harbin

Sea of Japan (East Sea)

Akita

Honshu

Sendai

Kyakhta

Da Hinggan Ling

40° N

Ulan Bator

M O N G O L I A

Hovd

Altay

Gobi Desert

100° E

110° E

130° E

130° E

140° E

Flag	Country	Capital
	Armenia F2	Capital : Yerevan
	Azerbaijan F2	Capital : Baku
	Georgia F2	Capital : Tbilisi
	Kazakhstan H2	Capital : Astana
	Russia H4	Capital : Moscow

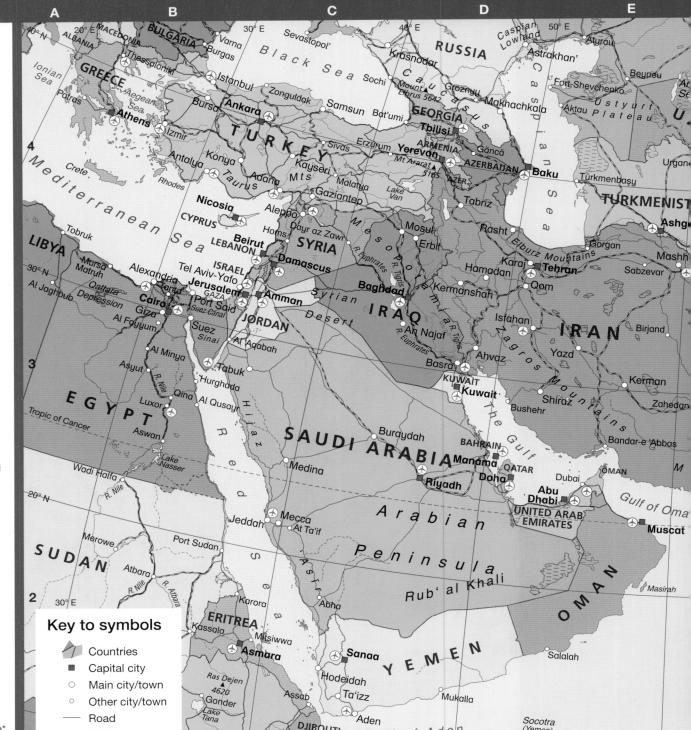

Afghanistan F4
Capital : Kabul

Bahrain E3
Capital : Manama

Bangladesh H3
Capital : Dhaka

Bhutan I3
Capital : Thimphu

India G3
Capital : New Delhi

Iran E4
Capital : Tehran

Iraq D4
Capital : Baghdad

Israel C4
Capital : Jerusalem*

Jordan C4
Capital : Amman

Kuwait D3
Capital : Kuwait

Kyrgyzstan G5
Capital : Bishkek

Lebanon C4
Capital : Beirut

Nepal H3
Capital : Kathmandu

Oman E2
Capital : Muscat

Pakistan F3
Capital : Islamabad

Qatar E3
Capital : Doha

Saudi Arabia D3
Capital : Riyadh

* Internationally disputed capital.

Key to symbols

- Countries
- ■ Capital city
- ○ Main city/town
- ◦ Other city/town
- — Road
- ─ Railway
- Canal
- ✈ Airport
- Lake
- Seasonal lake
- River
- Mount Everest ▲ 8848   Mountain and height in metres

0   200   400   600   800 km

Scale : One centimetre on this map is the same as 200 kilometres on the ground.

Sri Lanka H1
Capital : Sri Jayewardenepura Kotte

Syria C4
Capital : Damascus

Tajikistan F4
Capital : Dushanbe

Turkmenistan E4
Capital : Ashgabat

United Arab Emirates E3
Capital : Abu Dhabi

Uzbekistan F5
Capital : Tashkent

Yemen D2
Capital : Sanaa

Key to symbols

Countries	Canal
Capital city	Airport
Main city/town	Lake
Other city/town	Seasonal lake
Road	River
Railway	Gongga Shan Mountain and height in metres 7556

Gonga Shan ▲ 7556

RUSSIA

MONGOLIA

Ulan Bator

Gobi Desert

CHINA

KAZAKHSTAN

INDIA

MYANMAR (BURMA)
Nay Pyi Taw

THAILAND

LAOS
Vientiane

VIETNAM
Hanoi
Hai Phong

NORTH KOREA
Pyongyang

SOUTH KOREA
Seoul

JAPAN
Tokyo
Yokohama

TAIWAN
Taipei
China claims Taiwan as its 23rd province

Altai Mountains
Da Hinggan Ling
Sikhote-Alin

Lake Baikal

Sea of Japan (East Sea)
Yellow Sea
East China Sea
South China Sea
Bo Hai
PACIFIC OCEAN
Ryukyu Islands
Gulf of Tongking
Luzon Strait
Taiwan Strait

Hainan
Luzon
Hokkaido
Honshu
Shikoku
Kyushu
Sakhalin
Kuril'sk
Northern Mariana Islands (USA)

Huang He
Chang Jiang
R. Amur
R. Mekong
R. Irrawaddy
Salween
Qinghai Hu
Dongting Hu
Lop Nur

Irkutsk, Ulan-Ude, Chita, Sretensk, Svobodnyy, Blagoveshchensk, Khabarovsk, Komsomol'sk-na-Amure, Nikolayevsk, Aleksandrovsk-Sakhalinskiy, Yuzhno-Sakhalinsk, Korsakov, Poronaysk, Kholmsk, Kushiro

Ürümqi, Korla, Karamay, Altay, Hovd, Ulaangom, Zavan, Tuvan, Kyakhta, Borzya, Manzhouli, Hailar, Qiqihar, Daqing, Fuyu, Harbin, Jiamusi, Jixi, Yichun, Changchun, Jilin, Fushun, Shenyang, Anshan, Fuxin, Dandong

Nagqu, Lhasa, Golmud, Qamdo, Njingchi, Panzhihua, Chuxiong, Kunming, Kaiyuan, Chengdu, Leshan, Yibin, Luzhou, Chongqing, Guiyang, Nanning, Yulin, Zhanjiang, Haikou

Beijing, Tianjin, Tangshan, Datong, Baotou, Hohhot, Yinchuan, Lanzhou, Xining, Tianshui, Xi'an, Hanzhong, Luoyang, Zhengzhou, Kaifeng, Shijiazhuang, Handan, Taiyuan, Jinan, Qingdao, Yantai, Weifang, Lianyungang, Heze, Xuzhou, Suzhou, Huainan, Hefei, Nanjing, Wuhu, Nanchang, Wuhan, Changsha, Hengyang, Guangzhou, Shenzhen, Hong Kong, Macao, Shantou, Xiamen, Fuzhou, Wenzhou, Ningbo, Hangzhou, Shanghai

Vladivostok, Nakhodka, Chongjin, Kimchaek, Hamhung, Hungnam, Daejeon, Daegu, Busan, Gwangju

Sapporo, Hakodate, Aomori, Hachinohe, Akita, Sendai, Niigata, Kanazawa, Nagoya, Kyoto, Osaka, Kobe, Kochi, Kumamoto, Kagoshima, Nagasaki, Fukuoka, Hiroshima, Naha, Okinawa

Mount Fuji 3776

0 200 400 600 800 km

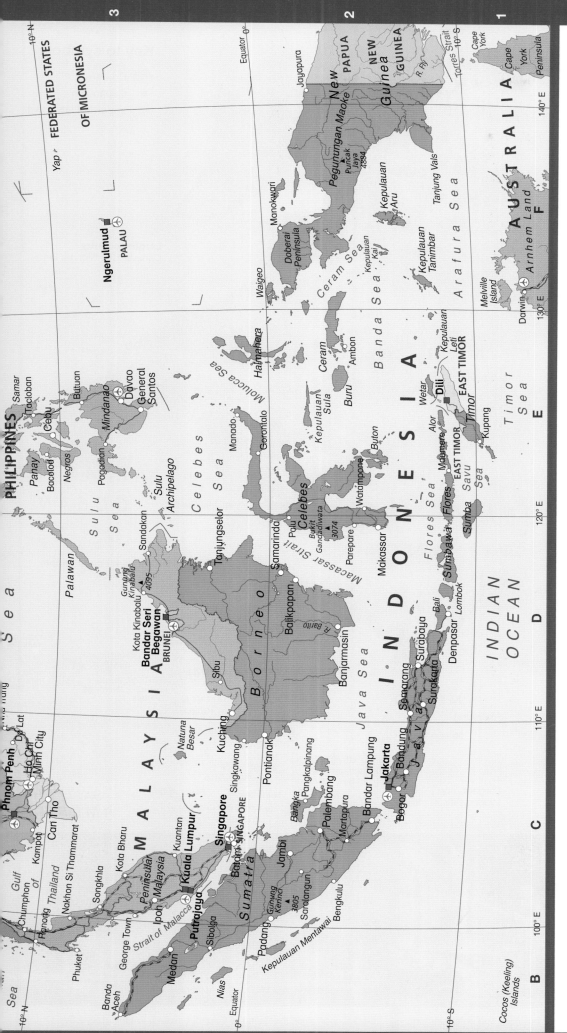

Mongolia B7
Capital :
Ulan Bator

Vietnam C4
Capital : Hanoi

Malaysia C3
Capital :
Putrajaya/
Kuala Lumpur

Thailand B4
Capital : Bangkok

Laos C4
Capital : Vientiane

Taiwan E5
Capital : Taipei

Japan G6
Capital : Tokyo

South Korea E6
Capital : Seoul

Indonesia D2
Capital : Jakarta

Singapore C3
Capital : Singapore

East Timor E2
Capital : Dili

Philippines E4
Capital : Manila

China B6
Capital : Beijing

Palau F3
Capital : Ngerulmud

Cambodia C4
Capital :
Phnom Penh

North Korea E7
Capital :
Pyongyang

Brunei D3
Capital : Bandar
Seri Begawan

Myanmar B4
Capital :
Nay Pyi Taw

Total population
of North America
582 million

ARCTIC
OCEAN

N
W E
S

GREENLAND
(Denmark)

Baffin
Bay

Key to symbols

Countries
■ Capital city
○ Important city/town

ALASKA
U.S.A.

○ Anchorage

Nuuk
(Godthåb) ■

Largest country
Canada 10 million sq km

○ Iqaluit

Great Bear
Lake

Great Slave
Lake

Hudson
Bay

C A N A D A

St John's ○

○ Edmonton

○ Calgary

Québec ○
Montréal ○

Halifax ○

Vancouver ○

Winnipeg ○

Lake
Huron
Ottawa ■

Seattle ○

Lake
Superior

Toronto ○

Lake
Ontario

Boston ○

PACIFIC

Portland ○

Minneapolis ○

Lake
Michigan

Detroit ○

Lake
Erie

New York ○

ATLANTIC

OCEAN

Chicago ○
Pittsburgh ○

Washington D.C. ■

OCEAN

Sacramento ○

U N I T E D   S T A T E S

Salt Lake
City ○

Denver ○

Kansas
City ○

St Louis ○

San
Francisco ○

Bermuda
(UK)

O F   A M E R I C A

Country with most people
USA 324 million

Los Angeles ○
San Diego ○

Phoenix ○

Dallas ○

Atlanta ○

El Paso ○

Houston ○

New Orleans ○

Miami ○

THE
BAHAMAS

ANTIGUA AND
BARBUDA

Nassau ■

DOMINICAN
REPUBLIC

PUERTO
RICO
(USA)

DOMINICA

ST LUCIA

Gulf of
Mexico

Havana ■

CUBA

HAITI
Port-au-
Prince

Santo
Domingo

BARBA

Monterrey ○

GRENADA

M E X I C O

JAMAICA
Kingston ■

Caribbean   Sea

Guadalajara ○

Belmopan ■

The British Isles
at the same scale.

Mexico City ■

Puebla ○

BELIZE
GUATEMALA
Guatemala City ■
San Salvador ■
EL SALVADOR

HONDURAS
Tegucigalpa ■
NICARAGUA
Managua ■

Panama City ■

SOUTH

Largest city
Mexico City 22 million

San José ■
COSTA RICA

PANAMA

AMERICA

Manhattan, at the heart of New York, is a centre for business and entertainment.

The U.S. Congress meets in the Capitol building, Washington D.C.

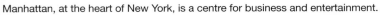

0   400   800   1200   1600   2000 km

Scale : One centimetre on this map is the same as 400 kilometres on the ground.

Total area of
North America
25 million sq km

**ARCTIC
OCEAN**

N
W E
S

Greenland

EUROPE

Iceland

*Baffin
Bay*

*Victoria
Island*

Davis Strait

Baffin Island

Largest island
Greenland 2 million sq km

Cape Farewell

R. Yukon

▲ *Denali
6190*

*Gulf of
Alaska*

▲ *Mount Logan
5959*

*Great Bear
Lake*

*Great Slave
Lake*

R. Mackenzie

Labrador

Largest lake
Lake Superior 82 100 sq km

Highest mountain
Denali 6190 m

R. Peace

Rocky Mountains

*Hudson
Bay*

Newfoundland

**PACIFIC
OCEAN**

3954

Great Plains

Canadian Shield

R. St. Lawrence

Lake Superior

*Great
Lakes*

Lake Huron

Lake Ontario

Cape Cod

**ATLANTIC
OCEAN**

R. Snake

*Great Salt
Lake*

R. Missouri

*Lake
Michigan*

Niagara Falls

Lake Erie

Appalachian Mountains

*Great
Basin*

▲ *Mount
Elbert
4398*

R. North Platte

R. Ohio

▲ *Mount Whitney
4418*

R. Colorado

*Grand
Canyon*

2037

Longest river
Mississippi-Missouri 5969 km

R. Red

R. Mississippi

Gulf of California

Sierra Madre Occidental

R. Brazos

Rio Grande

Florida

Sierra Madre Oriental

*Gulf of
Mexico*

Cuba

Hispaniola

Yucatán

Caribbean Sea

▲ *Popocatépetl
5452*

*Lake
Nicaragua*

Isthmus of Panama

**SOUTH
AMERICA**

Ellesmere Island

Key to symbols

- 🗺 Lake
- 🗺 Seasonal lake
- 〜 River
- ▢ Polar ice cap
- *Denali*
  6190 ▲ Mountain and height in metres

Land height above
sea level in metres

over 5000	
2000 – 5000	
1000 – 2000	
500 – 1000	
200 – 500	
0 – 200	

The Grand Canyon, a wide, deep gorge in the southwest of the USA.

The Niagara Falls, a set of massive waterfalls in Canada and the USA.

0   400   800   1200   1600   2000 km

Scale : One centimetre on this map is the same as 400 kilometres on the ground.

Key to symbols

- ◹ Countries
- ■ Capital city
- ○ Main city/town
- ◦ Other city/town
- — Road
- ┼┼ Railway
- ～ Canal
- ✈ Airport
- ⬭ Lake
- ⬭ Seasonal lake
- ～ River
- Denali 6190 ▲ Mountain and height in metres

CO. CONNECTICUT
MASS. MASSACHUSETTS
N.H. NEW HAMPSHIRE
P.E.I. PRINCE EDWARD ISLAND
PENN. PENNSYLVANIA
R.I. RHODE ISLAND
VER. VERMONT

Scale : One centimetre on this map is the same as 170 kilometres on the ground.

0   200   400   600   800 km

PACIFIC OCEAN

Aleutian Islands
Platinum
Alaska Peninsula
Aleutian Range
Kodiak Island
Kodiak
Kenai
Seward
Anchorage
Glennallen
Gulf of Alaska
Alaska Range
Denali 6190 ▲
Fairbanks
U.S.A.
A L A S K A
Nome
Seward Peninsula
St. Lawrence Island
Point Hope
Arctic Circle
Brooks Range
Point Barrow
Barrow
Prudhoe Bay
Beaufort Sea
Inuvik
Fort McPherson
Fort Good Hope
R. Arctic Red
R. Mackenzie
Great Bear Lake
Banks Island
Victoria Island
Prince Patrick Island
Melville Island
Stefansson Island
Bathurst Inlet

Fort Yukon
R. Yukon
Dawson
Whitehorse
YUKON
Mackenzie Mountains
NORTHWEST TERRITORIES
C A N A D A
Yellowknife
Reliance
Great Slave Lake
Hay River
R. Taltson
R. Back

Skagway
Mount Fairweather 4670
Juneau
Alexander Archipelago
Ketchikan
Prince Rupert
Haida Gwaii (Queen Charlotte Islands)
Stewart
Kitimat
Ocean Falls
Coast Mountains
Mount Waddington 4042
BRITISH COLUMBIA
Mount Lloyd George 2972
Fort Nelson
Watson Lake
R. Stikine
R. Liard
R. Liard
Mount Logan 5959
R. Yukon

ROCKY MOUNTAINS
Dawson Creek
Prince George
Mount Robson 3954
R. Peace
Peace River
Fort Chipewyan
Lake Athabasca
Uranium City
R. Slave
La Ronge
R. Churchill
Reindeer Lake
Thompson
Flin Flon
MAN
The Pas
Lake Winnipeg

Campbell River
Vancouver Island
Victoria
Vancouver
Kamloops
R. Fraser
Kelowna
Cranbrook
Jasper
Banff
Grande Prairie
Edmonton
ALBERTA
Lloydminster
Calgary
R. North Saskatchewan
Saskatoon
SASKATCHEWAN
Prince Albert
R. Saskatchewan
Winnipegosis
Lake Winnipegosis
Dauphin
Brandon
Winnipeg

Seattle
Olympia
WASHINGTON
Mount St. Helens 2550 ▲
Mount Rainier 4392 ▲
Spokane
Portland
Salem
Eugene
Cascade Range
R. Columbia
R. Snake
OREGON
La Grande
Boise
Coast Ranges
Crescent City
Klamath Falls
Redding
Mount Shasta 4317 ▲
Sacramento
San Francisco
Oakland
San Jose
Reno
Carson City
CALIFORNIA
NEVADA
Fresno
Mount Whitney 4418 ▲
Tonopah
Ely 3982
Great Wheeler Peak
Great Basin
UTAH
Great Salt Lake
Salt Lake City
Idaho Falls
R. Snake
Twin Falls
IDAHO
Bitterroot Range
Missoula
Great Falls
Helena
Shelby
Lethbridge
Medicine Hat
Moose Jaw
Regina
Lake Manitoba
MONTANA
R. Missouri
Billings
Glasgow
Miles City
Williston
Minot
NORTH DAKOTA
Bismarck
R. James
R. Yellowstone
Buffalo
WYOMING
Gannett Peak 4202 ▲
Casper
Green River
R. Green
COLORADO
Cheyenne
Rapid City
SOUTH DAKOTA
R. Cheyenne
R. North Platte
North Platte
NEBRASKA
Sioux Falls
UNITED STATES OF AMERICA
Omaha
Sioux City
R. Missouri

50° N
40° N
170° W
160° W
150° W
140° W
120° W
110° W
100° W
120° W
60° N
70° N
80° N
60° W

H I J K L M N O P Q

6 5 4

GREENLAND
(Denmark)

Baffin
Bay

Ellesmere Island

Devon
Island

Resolute

Somerset
Island

Arctic
Bay

Gulf of Boothia

Boothia
Peninsula

Baffin Island

Melville
Peninsula

Prince
Charles
Island

Repulse Bay

Foxe
Basin

Amadjuak
Lake

Iqaluit

Southampton
Island

Coral
Harbour

Mansel
Island

Coats
Island

Salluit

Hudson Strait

Kangiqsujuaq

ICELAND

Seydisfjördhur
Höfn
Isafjördhur
Reykjavik

Arctic Circle

Gunnbjorn Fjeld
3700

Denmark Strait

Tasiilaq

Kong Christian IX Land

Kong Frederik VI Kyst

Cape Farewell

Nanortalik

**Nuuk
(Godthåb)**

Labrador
Sea

NEWFOUNDLAND AND LABRADOR

**ATLANTIC
OCEAN**

3

2

1

Qaanaaq

Cape
Parry

Clyde River

Pangnirtung

Davis Strait

Saqqaq

Disko

Greenland
Capital : Nuuk

Canada
Capital : Ottawa

D A

Churchill

Hudson
Bay

Fort Severn

Belcher
Islands

Inukjuak

Kangiqsualujjuaq

R. George

Kuujjuaq

Hopedale

Smallwood
Reservoir

Port Hope
Simpson

St Anthony

Happy Valley-
Goose Bay

Scheffersville

Labrador

R. Churchill

Labrador City

Lac
Caniapiscau

Réservoir
La Grande 2

Chisasibi

Réservoir
La Grande 3

R. Eastmain

QUEBEC

Grand Falls-
Windsor

St John's

Newfoundland

Channel-Port
aux-Basques

St Pierre
and Miquelon
(France)

Havre-St-Pierre

Eastmain

Lac Mistassini

Sept-Îles

Baie-Comeau

Gulf of
St Lawrence

Sydney

Cape Breton
Island

ONTARIO

R. Albany

Fort
Albany

Moosonee

R. Moose

R. Harricana

Chibougamau

Chicoutimi

Jonquière

R. St Lawrence

Bathurst

P.E.I.

Charlottetown

Sandy Lake

Sioux
Lookout

Lake
Nipigon

Nipigon

Longlac

Timmins

La Sarre

Val-d'Or

Rivière-du-Loup

**NEW
BRUNSWICK**

Moncton

Saint
John

**NOVA
SCOTIA**

Cape Breton
Island

Frances

Thunder Bay

Chapleau

Québec

Sherbrooke

Mount
Washington
1918

Halifax

Cape Sable

Fort
Frances

Lake Superior

Sault
Sainte Marie

Sudbury

North
Bay

Trois-Rivières

Montréal

MAINE

Augusta

Portland

Yarmouth

Duluth

Escanaba

Lake Michigan

Lake Huron

R. Ottawa

Ottawa

Kingston

VER

N.H.

Concord

Cape Cod

Minneapolis

St
Paul

Green Bay

Traverse
City

Oshawa

Lake Ontario

Toronto

Rochester

Albany

MASS

Boston

Providence

Long Island

WISCONSIN

MICHIGAN

Hamilton

Buffalo

Hartford

Milwaukee

Flint

Lansing

NEW YORK

Cedar
Rapids

Moines

Chicago

South
Bend

Detroit

Lake Erie

Erie

Cleveland

Toledo

PENN.

Allentown

New York

Des

TES

SOTA

A

J K L M

PACIFIC OCEAN

CANADA

BRITISH COLUMBIA
ALBERTA
SASKATCHEWAN
MANITOBA

Vancouver Island
Victoria
Vancouver
Kelowna
Cranbrook
Calgary
Swan River
Dauphin
Lake Winnipeg
Lake Manitoba
▲3285 Mount Baker
Seattle
Sandpoint
Medicine Hat
Lethbridge
Moose Jaw
Regina
Brandon
Winnipeg
Olympia
WASHINGTON
▲4392 Mount Rainier
Ellensburg
Spokane
Kalispell
Shelby
Estevan
Mount St Helens ▲2550
Portland
Richland
R. Snake
R. Columbia
R. St Joe
Missoula
Great Falls
R. Missouri
Glasgow
Williston
Minot
R. Sheyenne
Grand Forks
Salem
OREGON
La Grande
R. Columbia
R. Salmon
MONTANA
Helena
Butte
Billings
R. Yellowstone
Miles City
NORTH DAKOTA
Bismarck
R. James
Fargo
MI
Eugene
Cascade Range
Bend
ROCKY
Bitterroot Range
BE
Coast Ranges
Crescent City
Burns
IDAHO
Boise
Buffalo
SOUTH DAKOTA
Aberdeen
Eureka
Mount Shasta ▲4317
Redding
Klamath Falls
Idaho Falls
Gannett Peak ▲4202
Lander
Casper
Rapid City
R. Cheyenne
Pierre
Brookings
M
Ukiah
Winnemucca
R. Humboldt
Twin Falls
R. Snake
MOUNTAINS
WYOMING
Green River
Rawlins
Cheyenne
R. Missouri
Sioux Falls
Sierra Nevada
Reno
NEVADA
Elko
Great Salt Lake
Salt Lake City
NEBRASKA
Sioux City
Sacramento
San Francisco
Carson City
Great Basin
Ely
Green River
R. Green
Denver
R. North Platte
Sterling
North Platte
R. Platte
Omaha
Lincoln
Oakland
San Jose
▲3982 Wheeler Peak
UTAH
Richfield
Grand Junction
UNITED
Colorado Springs
Burlington
E
Kansas City
Salinas
Mount Whitney ▲4418
Death Valley
Tonopah
Cedar City
R. Colorado
COLORADO
Pueblo
R. Arkansas
Junction City
Independence
San Luis Obispo
CALIFORNIA
Fresno
Bakersfield
Las Vegas
Monte Vista
Trinidad
▲4011 Wheeler Peak
KANSAS
Dodge City
Wichita
OF
A
M
Arkansas City
Point Conception
Oxnard
Los Angeles
Riverside
Santa Ana
Needles
R. Colorado
Grand Canyon
Grand Canyon
Flagstaff
Colorado Plateau
Santa Fe
R. Canadian
Amarillo
OKLAHOMA
Clinton
Oklahoma City
Tulsa
Fort S
San Diego
Tijuana
Mexicali
Yuma
R. Gila
Phoenix
ARIZONA
Albuquerque
NEW MEXICO
Clovis
Wichita Falls
R. Red
Ensenada
Picacho del Diablo ▲3096
San Felipe
Nogales
R. Gila
Tucson
Baldy Peak ▲3476
Silver City
Artesia
Lubbock
R. Brazos
Abilene
Fort Worth
Dallas
Lázaro Cárdenas
Caborca
Nogales
El Paso
Ciudad Juárez
Midland
TEXAS
Waco
Guadalupe (Mexico)
Gulf of California
R. Sonora
Hermosillo
Sierra Madre Occidental
Pecos
R. Pecos
Edwards Plateau
R. Colorado
Austin
Houston
Punta Eugenia
Baja California
R. Yaqui
Guaymas
Ojinaga
Chihuahua
Piedras Negras
Del Rio
San Antonio
Gal
PACIFIC OCEAN
Santa Rosalía
Ciudad Obregón
MEXICO
Hidalgo del Parral
Jiménez
Monclova
Rio Grande
R. Salado
Laredo
Nuevo Laredo
Corpus Christi
Villa Insurgentes
Los Mochis
Culiacán
Torreón
R. Nazas
Saltillo
Sierra Madre Oriental
Monterrey
Reynosa
Matamoros
La Paz
Durango
Cerro Peña Nevada ▲3644
Ciudad Victoria
Tropic of Cancer
Cabo Falso
San José del Cabo
Mazatlán

125° W 120° W 115° W 110° W 105° W 100° W 95
50° N 45° N 40° N 35° N 30° N 25° N

N W E S

Scale : One centimetre on this map is the same as 120 kilometres on the ground.
0   200   400   600   800 km

H I J K L M N

90° W   85° W   80° W   75° W   70° W   65° W

6

Lake
Lout
Lake
Nipigon
Moosonee
R. Albany
R. Moose
R. Harricana
Matagami
Chibougamau
Baie-Comeau
Réservoir
Gouin
Rimouski
Bathurst
P.E.I.
NEW
BRUNSWICK
Moncton

ONTARIO
Longlac
Hearst
Nipigon
Marathon
Michipicoten
River
Chapleau
Timmins
Val-d'Or
La Sarre
QUÉBEC
Jonquière
Chicoutimi
R. St Lawrence
Rivière-du-Loup
R. St John
Québec
Presque
Isle
Montcton
Truro   45° N
Saint John
NOVA
SCOTIA

Thunder Bay
Isle Royale
Lake Superior
Sault Sainte
Marie
Sudbury
North Bay
R. Ottawa
Trois-Rivières
Montréal
Sherbrooke
Mount
Washington
1918
MAINE
Bangor
Halifax
Yarmouth
Cape Sable

5

TA
Duluth
Superior
WISCONSIN
Escanaba
Marquette
Green Bay
Lake Michigan
Lake Huron
Traverse City
MICHIGAN
Orillia
Oshawa
L. Ontario
Toronto
Hamilton
Kingston
Rochester
Montpelier
VER.
N.H.
Concord
Portland
Augusta
Cape Cod
Boston
Providence

eapolis
St Paul
R. Mississippi
bert Lea
Eau
Claire
Madison
Milwaukee
Grand
Rapids
Flint
Lansing
Detroit
Windsor
Lake Erie
Buffalo
Erie
NEW YORK
Albany
Hartford
MASS.
R. Hudson
R. Connecticut
CO.
Providence
40° N

Cedar
Rapids
R. Cedar
Rockford
R. Illinois
Chicago
South
Bend
Fort Wayne
Toledo
Cleveland
PENNSYLVANIA
Harrisburg
Allentown
Trenton
New York
Long Island

Iowa
City
Des
oines
ILLINOIS
INDIANA
OHIO
Columbus
Pittsburgh
NEW JERSEY
Philadelphia

4

TA
R. Mississippi
Bloomington
Springfield
Indianapolis
Cincinnati
R. Ohio
**WEST
VIRGINIA**
MARYLAND
Baltimore
Dover
DELAWARE

ferson
City
R. Missouri
St Louis
R. Wabash
Louisville
Lexington
Charleston
VIRGINIA
Washington D.C.
Alexandria
Salisbury

R. Ohio
KENTUCKY
Richmond
Norfolk

SSOURI
R. White
Springfield
Poplar Bluff
Nashville
Knoxville
Mt Mitchell
2037
Appalachian Mountains
Greensboro
Raleigh
NORTH CAROLINA
Cape Hatteras
35° N

3

Little
Rock
Memphis
Chattanooga
R. Tennessee
Greenville
Charlotte
Fayetteville
Wilmington
Cape Fear

KANSAS
Bristol
TENNESSEE
**SOUTH
CAROLINA**
Columbia

kana
eveport
Greenville
Tuscaloosa
Birmingham
Atlanta
Augusta
Charleston

Jackson
ALABAMA
Columbus
Montgomery
GEORGIA
Savannah

OUISIANA
MISSISSIPPI
R. Tombigbee
R. Alabama
Dothan
Valdosta
Savannah
**ATLANTIC
OCEAN**
30° N

2

xandria
Baton
Rouge
Mobile
Tallahassee
Lake City
Jacksonville

Lafayette
mont
Morgan
City
New Orleans
Mississippi
Delta
Daytona Beach
Cape Canaveral

FLORIDA
Orlando

Gulf of Mexico
St Petersburg
Tampa
Lake
Okeechobee
West Palm Beach
Fort Lauderdale
Miami
Grand
Bahama
Freeport
City
Great Abaco
**THE
BAHAMAS**
Nassau
New
Providence
Cat Island
Long Island
Tropic of Cancer
25° N

1

Florida Keys
Andros
Great Exuma
Turks and
Caicos Islands
(UK)

Straits of Florida
Acklins
Island
Grand Turk

Havana
Matanzas
Santa Clara
CUBA
Great
Inagua
20° N

Pinar del Rio
Camagüey

90° W   85° W   80° W   75° W

H I J K L

Key to symbols

Countries
■ Capital city
○ Main city/town
○ Other city/town
— Road
Railway
Canal
✈ Airport
Lake
Seasonal
lake
River
Mount
Whitney ▲ Mountain and
4418   height in metres

CO.   CONNECTICUT
MASS. MASSACHUSETTS
N.H.   NEW HAMPSHIRE
P.E.I. PRINCE EDWARD ISLAND
R.I.   RHODE ISLAND
VER.   VERMONT

United States of America
Capital : Washington D.C.

A B C D E F

UNITED STATES OF AMERICA

San Diego, Tijuana, Mexicali, Yuma, Phoenix, Tucson, Nogales, Ensenada, Picacho del Diablo 3096, Lázaro Cárdenas, San Felipe, Caborca, Silver City, El Paso, Ciudad Juárez, Artesia, Lubbock, Wichita Falls, Abilene, Fort Worth, Dallas, Texarkana, Greenville, Little Rock, ARKANSAS, MISSISSIPPI, Tuscaloosa, Jackson, Shreveport, Alexandria, Lafayette, Morgan City, Baton Rouge, Mobile, New Orleans

NEW MEXICO, ARIZONA, TEXAS, LOUISIANA

Midland, Pecos, R. Pecos, Edwards Plateau, Emory Peak 2389, Del Rio, Austin, Waco, San Antonio, Houston, Beaumont, Galveston, Corpus Christi

Hermosillo, Guaymas, Ciudad Obregón, Santa Rosalía, Los Mochis, Culiacán, Chihuahua, Jiménez, Hidalgo del Parral, Monclova, Piedras Negras, Nuevo Laredo, Laredo, Reynosa, Matamoros, Ojinaga

MEXICO

Baja California, Gulf of California, Sierra Madre Occidental, Sierra Madre Oriental, Punta Eugenia, Villa Insurgentes, Tropic of Cancer, La Paz, Cabo Falso, San José del Cabo, Mazatlán, Durango, Torreón, Saltillo, Monterrey, Cerro Peña Nevada 3644, Ciudad Victoria, Gulf of Mexico

Islas Revillagigedo (Mexico), Aguascalientes, Tepic, Puerto Vallarta, Guadalajara, Irapuato, León, Querétaro, San Luis Potosí, Ciudad de Valles, Tampico, Poza Rica, Mérida, Yucatán, Campeche

Colima, Morelia, Toluca, Mexico City, Cuernavaca, Popocatépetl 5452, Puebla, Orizaba, Veracruz, Coatzacoalcos, Bay of Campeche, Chetumal, Escárcega, Villahermosa, Belmopan, BELIZE

Lázaro Cárdenas, Acapulco, Sierra Madre del Sur, Oaxaca, Puerto Ángel, Juchitán, Gulf of Tehuantepec, Tuxtla Gutiérrez, GUATEMALA, Guatemala City, San Pedro, Santa Ana, San Salvador, EL SALVADOR, Tegucigalpa, HONDURAS, San Miguel

PACIFIC OCEAN

Key to symbols

- Countries
- Capital city
- Main city/town
- Other city/town
- Road
- Railway
- Canal
- Airport
- Lake
- Seasonal lake
- River
- Mountain and height in metres — Sierra Nevada del Cocuy 5493

Antigua and Barbuda L3 Capital: St John's
The Bahamas I5 Capital: Nassau
Barbados M2 Capital: Bridgetown
Belize G3 Capital: Belmopan
Costa Rica G2 Capital: San José
Cuba H4 Capital: Havana
Dominica L3 Capital: Roseau
Dominican Republic J3 Capital: Santo Domingo
El Salvador G2 Capital: San Salvador
Grenada L2 Capital: St George's

0 200 400 600 800 km

Scale: One centimetre on this map is the same as 135 kilometres on the ground.

Guatemala F3	Haiti J3	Honduras G2	Jamaica I3	Mexico D4	Nicaragua G2	Panama H1	St Kitts and Nevis L3	St Lucia L2	St Vincent and the Grenadines L2
Capital : Guatemala City	Capital : Port-au-Prince	Capital : Tegucigalpa	Capital : Kingston	Capital : Mexico City	Capital : Managua	Capital : Panama City	Capital : Basseterre	Capital : Castries	Capital : Kingstown

Total population of South America
424 million

Caribbean Sea

ATLANTIC
OCEAN

NORTH
AMERICA

Barranquilla · Maracaibo · **Caracas** · **Port of Spain**
TRINIDAD
AND TOBAGO

VENEZUELA

Medellín ·

Georgetown
Paramaribo
Cayenne

Largest country
Brazil 9 million sq km

Bogotá

GUYANA

SURINAME
FRENCH
GUIANA

COLOMBIA

Cali ·

Country with most people
Brazil 209 million

Quito

Belém ·

Galapagos Islands
(Ecuador)

ECUADOR

Guayaquil ·

São Luís ·

Fortaleza ·

Iquitos ·

Manaus ·

B R A Z I L

Natal ·

Trujillo ·

PERU

Recife ·

PACIFIC

Lima

Aracaju ·

OCEAN

Lake
Titicaca

Salvador ·

BOLIVIA

Brasília

Arequipa ·

La Paz

Sucre

Belo Horizonte ·

Antofagasta ·

PARAGUAY

Rio de
Janeiro

Largest city
São Paulo 22 million

Asunción

São Paulo ·

C
H
I
L
E

Curitiba ·

ATLANTIC

A
R
G
E
N
T
I
N
A

OCEAN

Juan Fernandez Islands
(Chile)

Porto Alegre ·

Valparaíso ·

URUGUAY

Santiago

Buenos
Aires

Montevideo

Concepción ·

Mar del Plata ·

Key to symbols

Falkland Islands (UK)
Claimed by Argentina

Countries

Punta
Arenas ·

Capital city

Tierra
del
Fuego

South Georgia and
South Sandwich
Islands (UK)
Claimed by Argentina

The British Isles
at the same scale.

Important city/town

Rio de Janeiro is the second-largest city in Brazil.

The ruins of the lost Inca city of Machu Picchu in Peru.

0 400 800 1200 1600 2000 km

Scale : One centimetre on this map is the same as 400 kilometres on the ground.

Caribbean Sea

NORTH AMERICA

ATLANTIC OCEAN

N
W E
S

Total area of South America
18 million sq km

Lake Maracaibo

Orinoco Delta

R. Orinoco

Llanos

Angel Falls

Mount Roraima ▲ 2810

Guiana Highlands

Mouths of the Amazon

R. Amazon

Longest river
River Amazon 6516 km

Galapagos Islands

R. Japurá

R. Negro

Amazon Basin

R. Amazon

Selvas

R. Madeira

R. Purus

R. São Francisco

R. Tocantins

Largest lake
Lake Titicaca 8340 sq km

A n d e s

Altiplano

Atacama Desert

Lake Titicaca

Brazilian Highlands

R. Paraguay

PACIFIC OCEAN

Gran Chaco

R. Salado

R. Paraná

Cerro Ojos del Salado ▲ 6893

Highest mountain
Aconcagua 6961 m

Aconcagua ▲ 6961

R. Paraná

R. Uruguay

Juan Fernandez Islands

Pampas

ATLANTIC OCEAN

Río de la Plata

R. Colorado

R. Negro

Valdes Peninsula

Isla de Chiloé

Patagonia

Largest island
Tierra del Fuego 47 000 sq km

Key to symbols

〜 Lake

〜 Seasonal lake

⁓ River

Aconcagua ▲ 6961   Mountain and height in metres

Land height above sea level in metres

over 5000
2000 – 5000
1000 – 2000
500 – 1000
200 – 500
0 – 200

Falkland Islands

Tierra del Fuego

Cape Horn

South Georgia

Wild horses in Patagonia, Chile.

The Amazon rainforest covers more than one third of Brazil.

0   400   800   1200   1600   2000 km

Scale : One centimetre on this map is the same as 400 kilometres on the ground.

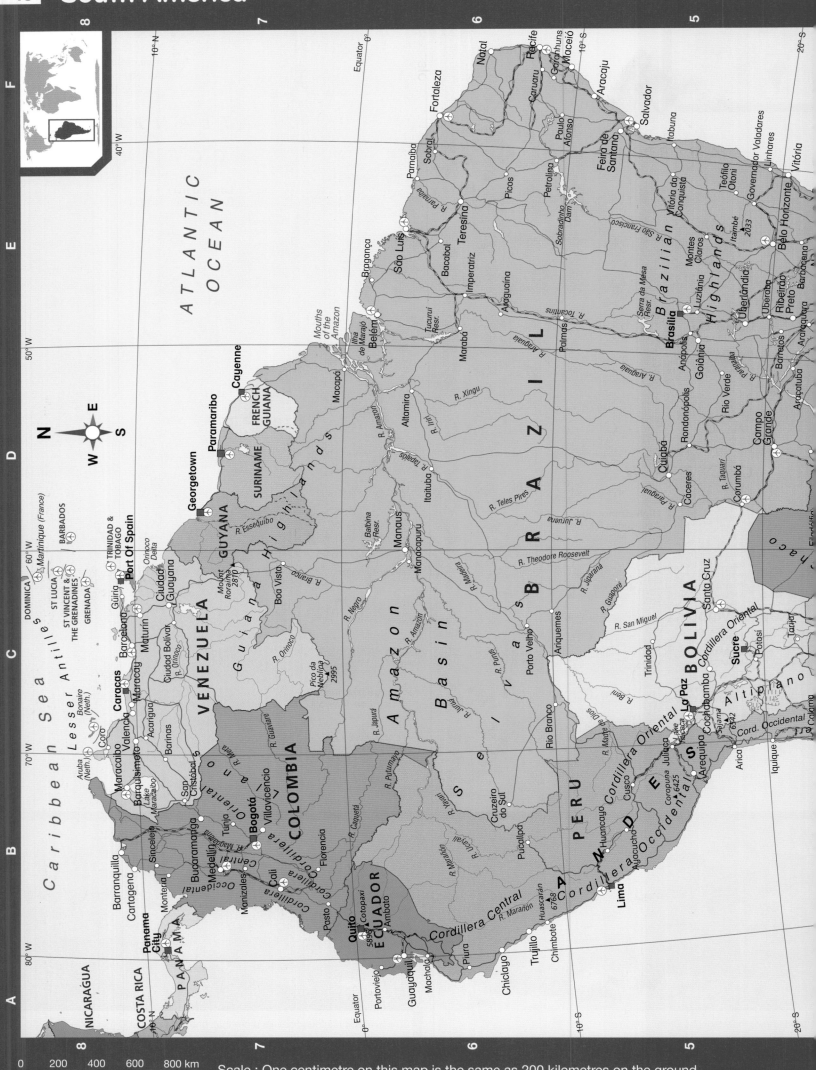

ATLANTIC OCEAN

Caribbean Sea

Lesser Antilles

DOMINICA
Martinique (France)
ST LUCIA
ST VINCENT & THE GRENADINES
BARBADOS
GRENADA
TRINIDAD & TOBAGO
Port Of Spain

NICARAGUA
COSTA RICA
PANAMA
Panama City

COLOMBIA
Bogotá
Cali
Medellín
Manizales
Pasto
Bucaramanga
Barrancabermeja
Tunja
Villavicencio
Florencia
Cúcuta
San Cristóbal
Cartagena
Barranquilla
Sincelejo
Montería

VENEZUELA
Caracas
Maracaibo
Valencia
Maracay
Barcelona
Barinas
Barquisimeto
Coro
Acarigua
Maturín
Ciudad Bolívar
Ciudad Guayana
Güiriá

GUYANA
Georgetown

SURINAME
Paramaribo

FRENCH GUIANA
Cayenne

Guiana Highlands
Mount Roraima 2810
Pico da Neblina 2995

ECUADOR
Quito
Guayaquil
Machala
Portoviejo
Ambato
Cotopaxi 5896

PERU
Lima
Trujillo
Chiclayo
Piura
Chimbote
Huancayo
Cusco
Arequipa
Ayacucho
Pucallpa
Cruzeiro do Sul
Huascarán 6768
Coropuna 6425

BOLIVIA
La Paz
Sucre
Santa Cruz
Cochabamba
Potosí
Trinidad
Oruro
Tarija
Lake Titicaca
Altiplano
Sajama 6542

BRAZIL
Brasília
Belém
Manaus
Fortaleza
Recife
Salvador
Belo Horizonte
Natal
Maceió
Aracaju
Teresina
São Luís
Macapá
Boa Vista
Porto Velho
Rio Branco
Campo Grande
Cuiabá
Goiânia
Uberlândia
Uberaba
Ribeirão Preto
Araçatuba
Campinas
Vitória
João Pessoa
Caruaru
Garanhuns
Petrolina
Feira de Santana
Vitória da Conquista
Itabuna
Governador Valadares
Linhares
Teófilo Otoni
Montes Claros
Luziânia
Anápolis
Rio Verde
Rondonópolis
Cáceres
Corumbá
Imperatriz
Marabá
Altamira
Santarém
Manacapuru
Araguaína
Palmas
Picos
Sobral
Parnaíba
Bacabal
Bragança
Sobradinho Dam
Tucuruí Resr.
Balbina Resr.
Serra da Mesa Resr.
Itambé 2033
Barbacena
Barretos

Amazon Basin
Selvas
Brazilian Highlands
Gran Chaco

ANDES
Cordillera Oriental
Cordillera Occidental
Cordillera Central
Cord. Occidental

R. Amazon
R. Negro
R. Branco
R. Orinoco
Orinoco Delta
Mouths of the Amazon
Ilha de Marajó
R. Xingu
R. Tapajós
R. Teles Pires
R. Iriri
R. Tocantins
R. Araguaia
R. Madeira
R. Purus
R. Juruá
R. Javari
R. Ucayali
R. Marañón
R. Napo
R. Putumayo
R. Caquetá
R. Japurá
R. Yavarí
R. Guaviare
R. Meta
R. Guainía
R. Essequibo
R. Branco
R. Juruena
R. Theodore Roosevelt
R. Jiparaná
R. Guaporé
R. San Miguel
R. Beni
R. Mamoré
R. Madre de Dios
R. Paraguai
R. Taquari
R. São Francisco
R. Parnaíba
R. Magdalena

Equator
0°
10°N
10°S
20°S
80°W
70°W
60°W
50°W
40°W

N E S W

0   200   400   600   800 km

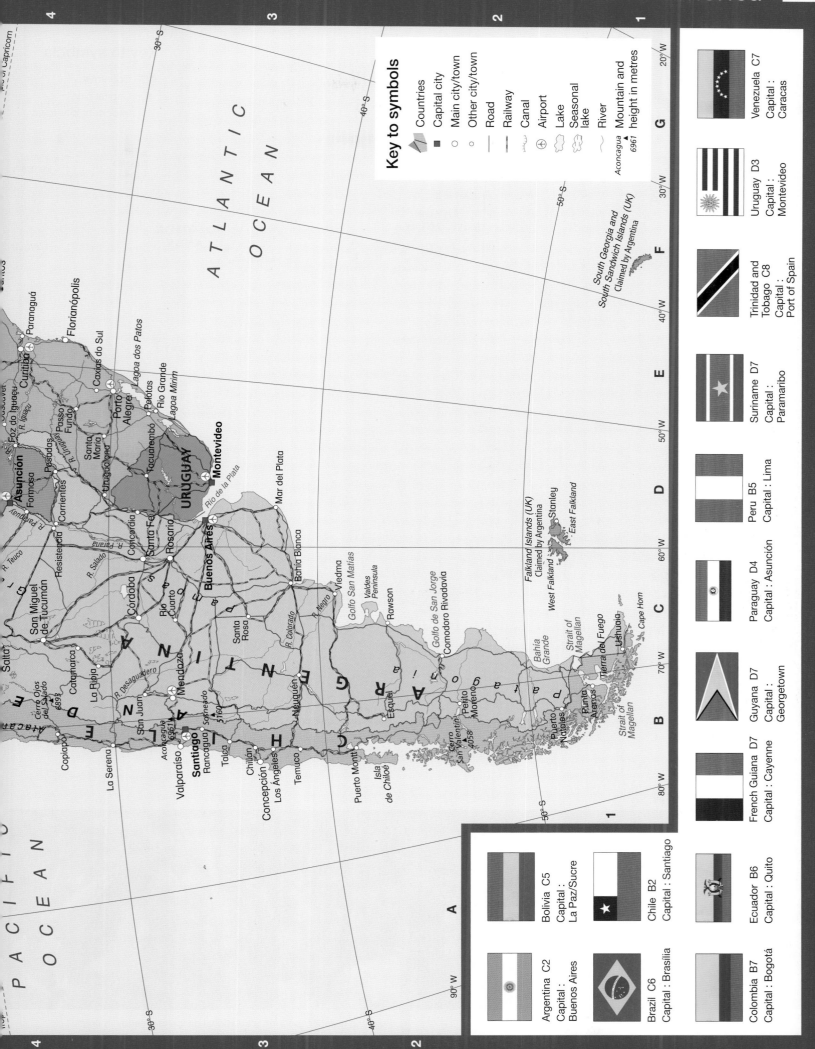

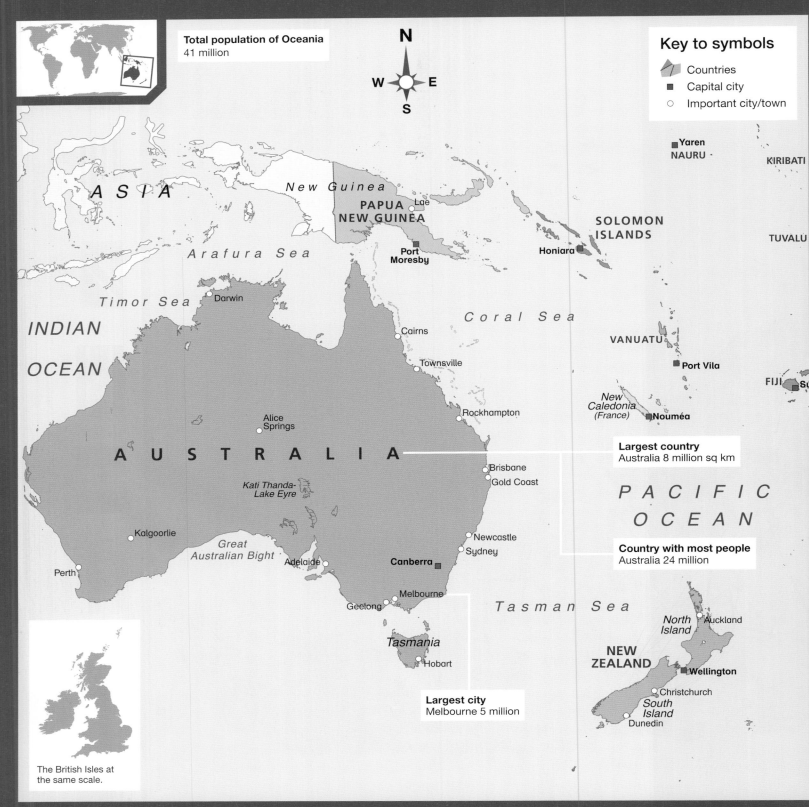

Total population of Oceania
41 million

N
W E
S

Key to symbols
◣ Countries
■ Capital city
○ Important city/town

Yaren
NAURU
KIRIBATI

ASIA

New Guinea

PAPUA
NEW GUINEA

Lae

SOLOMON
ISLANDS

TUVALU

Arafura Sea

Port
Moresby

Honiara

Timor Sea

Darwin

Coral Sea

INDIAN

OCEAN

Cairns

VANUATU

Townsville

Port Vila

Rockhampton

New
Caledonia
(France)

FIJI Suva

Alice
Springs

Nouméa

AUSTRALIA

Largest country
Australia 8 million sq km

PACIFIC
OCEAN

Kati Thanda-
Lake Eyre

Brisbane
Gold Coast

Kalgoorlie

Great
Australian Bight

Newcastle

Country with most people
Australia 24 million

Perth

Adelaide

Sydney

Canberra

Melbourne

Tasman Sea

Geelong

North
Island

Auckland

Tasmania

NEW
ZEALAND

Wellington

Hobart

Largest city
Melbourne 5 million

Christchurch
South
Island
Dunedin

The British Isles at
the same scale.

The harbour, bridge and opera house in Sydney.

Solomon Islanders perform a traditional dance to entertain tourists.

0   300   600   900   1200   1500 km

Scale : One centimetre on this map is the same as 325 kilometres on the ground.

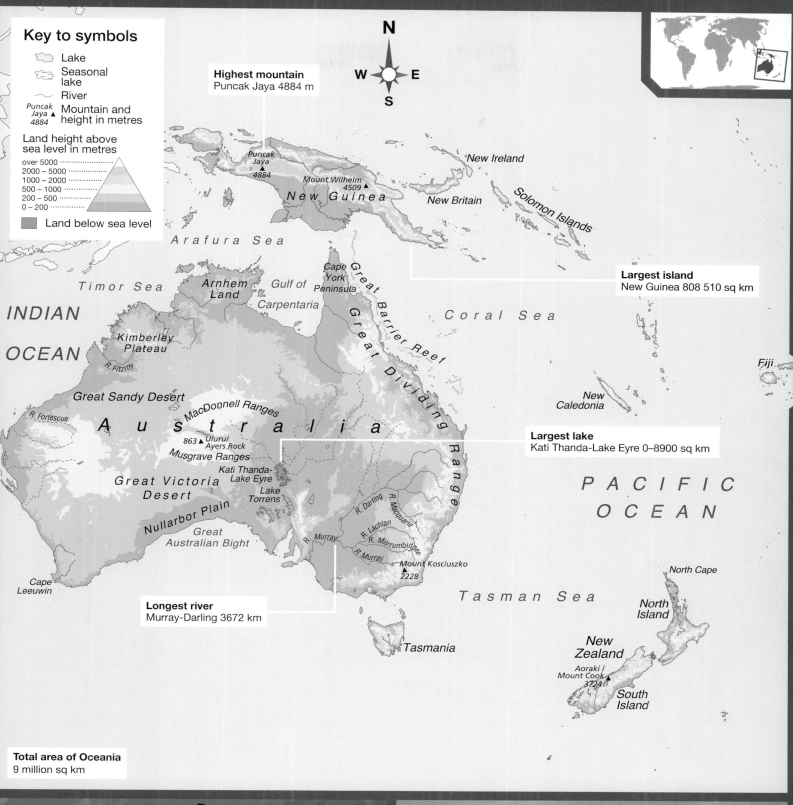

Key to symbols

- Lake
- Seasonal lake
- River
- Puncak Jaya ▲ 4884 Mountain and height in metres

Land height above sea level in metres

- over 5000
- 2000 – 5000
- 1000 – 2000
- 500 – 1000
- 200 – 500
- 0 – 200

Land below sea level

Highest mountain
Puncak Jaya 4884 m

N
W ☀ E
S

Puncak Jaya ▲ 4884

New Ireland

Mount Wilhelm 4509 ▲

New Guinea

New Britain

Solomon Islands

Arafura Sea

Largest island
New Guinea 808 510 sq km

Timor Sea

INDIAN

OCEAN

Arnhem Land

Gulf of Carpentaria

Cape York Peninsula

Great Barrier Reef

Coral Sea

Kimberley Plateau

R. Fitzroy

Great Sandy Desert

MacDonnell Ranges

Australia

Great Dividing Range

New Caledonia

Fiji

R. Fortescue

863 ▲ Ulurul Ayers Rock

Musgrave Ranges

Kati Thanda-Lake Eyre

Lake Torrens

Largest lake
Kati Thanda-Lake Eyre 0–8900 sq km

Great Victoria Desert

R. Darling
R. Macquarie
R. Lachlan
R. Murrumbidgee
R. Murray
R. Murray

PACIFIC

OCEAN

Nullarbor Plain

Great Australian Bight

Mount Kosciuszko 2228 ▲

North Cape

Cape Leeuwin

Tasman Sea

North Island

Longest river
Murray-Darling 3672 km

Tasmania

New Zealand

Aoraki / Mount Cook 3724 ▲

South Island

Total area of Oceania
9 million sq km

A diver feeds fish on the Great Barrier Reef, Australia.

Aoraki / Mount Cook, the highest mountain in New Zealand.

0   300   600   900   1200   1500 km

Scale : One centimetre on this map is the same as 325 kilometres on the ground.

Key to symbols

- Countries
- Capital city
- Main city/town
- Other city/town
- Road
- Railway
- Airport
- Lake
- Seasonal lake
- River
- Puncak Jaya ▲ 4884 Mountain and height in metres

Scale : One centimetre on this map is the same as 200 kilometres on the ground.

0 200 400 600 800 km

INDONESIA

Kepulauan Sula
Ceram
Ceram Sea
Buru
Ambon
Buton
Makassar
Kepulauan Kai
Kepulauan Aru
Banda Sea
Doberai Peninsula
Manokwari
Jayapura
Pegunungan Maoke
▲4884 Puncak Jaya
New Guinea
Kepulauan Tanimbar
Tanjung Vals
Flores Sea
Wetar
Alor
Maumere
Dili
EAST TIMOR
Timor
Kepulauan Leti
Sumbawa
Flores
Savu Sea
Kupang
Sumba

Admiralty Islands
Bismarck Sea
New Ireland
PAPUA NEW GUINEA
Mt Wilhelm ▲4509
Lae
New Britain
Bougainville Island
Solomon Sea
Kerema
Gulf of Papua
Port Moresby
D'Entrecasteaux Islands

Equator
Arafura Sea
Torres Strait
Cape York

Timor Sea

Darwin
Arnhem Land
Katherine
R. Daly
R. Victoria
Melville Island
Gulf of Carpentaria
Groote Eylandt
Wellesley Islands
Cape York Peninsula
R. Mitchell
Great Barrier Reef
Cairns

Coral Sea

Kimberley Plateau
Broome
Halls Creek
Tanami Desert
NORTHERN TERRITORY
Barkly Tableland
R. Flinders
Mount Isa
Great Dividing Range
Townsville
Mackay
Rockhampton

Great Sandy Desert
Port Hedland
R. Fortescue
Pilbara
Newman
Lake Disappointment
WESTERN AUSTRALIA
Lake Mackay
Mount Zeil 1531
MacDonnell Ranges
Alice Springs
Uluru/Ayers Rock ▲863
Simpson Desert
Cooper Creek
R. Diamantina
R. Warrego
QUEENSLAND
Barcaldine
Dirranbandi
Maryborough
Toowoomba
Brisbane
Gold Coast

Tropic of Capricorn
Gibson Desert
Musgrave Ranges
SOUTH AUSTRALIA
Kati Thanda-Lake Eyre (North)
Kati Thanda-Lake Eyre (South)
Bourke
Grafton

R. Murchison
Geraldton
Great Victoria Desert
Lake Torrens
Lake Gairdner
Broken Hill
Cobar
Dubbo
NEW SOUTH WALES
R. Darling
R. Lachlan
Tamworth
Port Macquarie
Newcastle
Bathurst
Sydney
Wollongong

Kalgoorlie
Nullarbor Plain
Port Augusta
Port Lincoln
Lake Torrens
Hay
R. Murrumbidgee
R. Murray
Wagga Wagga
Canberra
AUST. CAP. TER.

Perth
Fremantle
Norseman
Esperance
Great Australian Bight
Adelaide
Murray Bridge
Kangaroo Island
Horsham
VICTORIA
R. Murray
Mount Kosciuszko ▲2228
Great Dividing Range
Melbourne
Geelong
Mount Gambier
Bairnsdale

Cape Leeuwin
Albany

Bass Strait
TASMANIA
Burnie
Mount Ossa ▲1617
Hobart
South East Cape

Tasman Sea

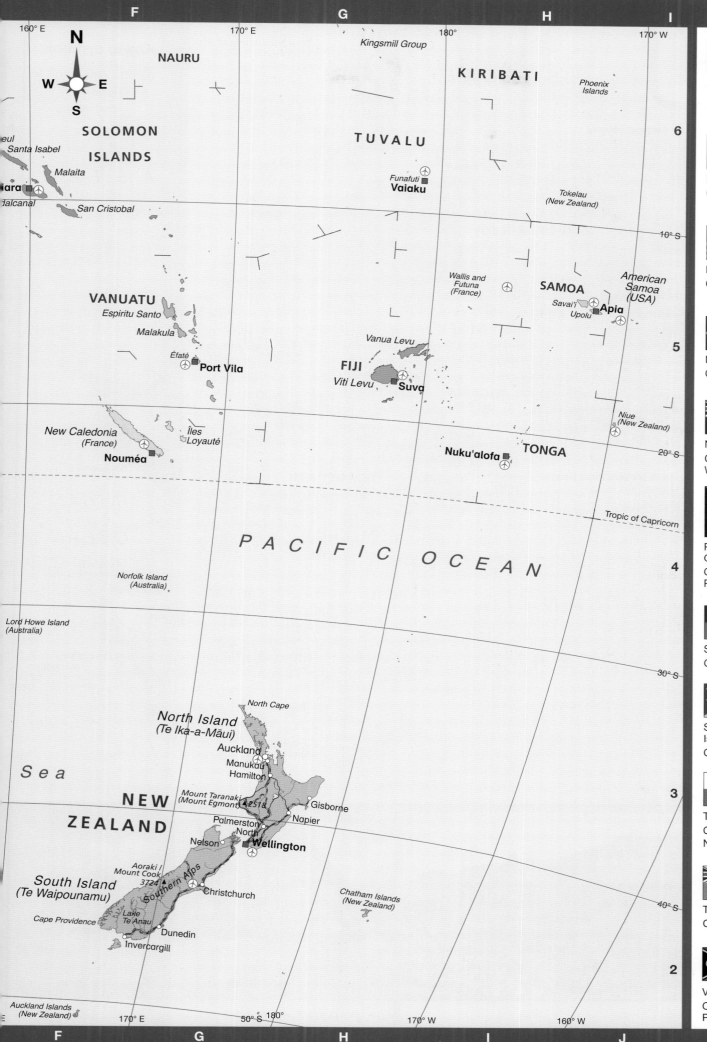

N
W E
S

160° E
170° E
180°
170° W

NAURU

KINGSMILL Group

KIRIBATI

SOLOMON
ISLANDS

TUVALU

Phoenix
Islands

6

eul
Santa Isabel

Malaita

iara

San Cristobal

Funafuti
Vaiaku

Tokelau
(New Zealand)

10° S

alcanal

VANUATU

Espiritu Santo

Malakula

Éfaté
Port Vila

Wallis and
Futuna
(France)

SAMOA

Savai'i
Upolu
Apia

American
Samoa
(USA)

5

Vanua Levu

FIJI

Viti Levu
Suva

New Caledonia
(France)

Îles
Loyauté

Nouméa

Niue
(New Zealand)

Nuku'alofa
TONGA

20° S

Tropic of Capricorn

PACIFIC OCEAN

4

Norfolk Island
(Australia)

Lord Howe Island
(Australia)

30° S

North Cape

North Island
(Te Ika-a-Māui)

Auckland

Manukau
Hamilton

S e a

NEW
ZEALAND

Mount Taranaki
(Mount Egmont) ▲ 2518

Gisborne

Napier

Palmerston
North

Nelson

Wellington

Aoraki /
Mount Cook

3724 ▲

Southern Alps

Christchurch

Chatham Islands
(New Zealand)

40° S

South Island
(Te Waipounamu)

Cape Providence

Lake
Te Anau

Dunedin

Invercargill

3

2

Auckland Islands
(New Zealand)

170° E
50° S
180°

170° W

160° W

F
G
H
I
J

Australia B4
Capital :
Canberra

Fiji G5
Capital : Suva

Kiribati H6
Capital : Bairiki

Nauru F6
Capital : Yaren

New Zealand G2
Capital :
Wellington

Papua New
Guinea D6
Capital :
Port Moresby

Samoa H5
Capital : Apia

Solomon
Islands F6
Capital : Honiara

Tonga H4
Capital :
Nuku'alofa

Tuvalu G6
Capital : Vaiaku

Vanuatu F5
Capital :
Port Vila

Largest country
Algeria 2 million sq km

Total population of Africa
1256 million

Key to symbols
◤ Countries
■ Capital city
○ Important city/town

Largest city
Cairo 21 million

Country with most people
Nigeria 191 million

EUROPE

ASIA

Mediterranean Sea

N
W E
S

Azores (Portugal)

Madeira (Portugal)

Algiers
Tunis
TUNISIA
Tripoli
Rabat
Casablanca
MOROCCO

Canary Is (Spain)

Laayoune
Western Sahara

ALGERIA

LIBYA

EGYPT

Alexandria
Giza Cairo
Benghazi

Red Sea

MAURITANIA
Nouakchott

MALI

NIGER

CHAD

SUDAN
Khartoum

ERITREA
Asmara

CAPE VERDE
Praia

Dakar
SENEGAL
THE GAMBIA
Banjul
GUINEA-BISSAU
Bissau
Bamako
BURKINA FASO
Ouagadougou
Niamey

Lake Chad
Ndjamena

DJIBOUTI
Djibouti

Conakry
GUINEA
Freetown
SIERRA LEONE
Monrovia
LIBERIA
CÔTE D'IVOIRE
Yamoussoukro
Abidjan
GHANA
Accra
Lomé
TOGO
BENIN
Porto-Novo
Lagos

NIGERIA
Abuja

CENTRAL AFRICAN REPUBLIC
Bangui

SOUTH SUDAN
Juba

ETHIOPIA
Addis Ababa

SOMALIA
Mogadishu

CAMEROON
Malabo
EQUATORIAL GUINEA
São Tomé
SÃO TOMÉ & PRÍNCIPE
Yaoundé
Libreville
GABON
CONGO
Brazzaville
Kinshasa

DEMOCRATIC REPUBLIC OF THE CONGO

UGANDA
Kampala
RWANDA
Kigali
BURUNDI
Bujumbura
Lake Victoria
KENYA
Nairobi
Dodoma
TANZANIA
Dar es Salaam
Mombasa

Lake Turkana

INDIAN OCEAN

SEYCHELLES
Victoria

Lake Tanganyika

Ascension Island (UK)

ATLANTIC

St Helena (UK)

OCEAN

Luanda

ANGOLA

ZAMBIA
Lusaka

MALAWI
Lilongwe
Lake Nyasa

Harare
ZIMBABWE

MOZAMBIQUE

Beira

Aldabra Is (Seychelles)

Moroni
COMOROS

Mayotte (France)

MADAGASCAR
Antananarivo

MAURITIUS
Réunion (France)
Port Louis

NAMIBIA
Windhoek
Walvis Bay

BOTSWANA
Gaborone

Pretoria
Johannesburg
Mbabane
Maputo
Lobamba
ESWATINI (SWAZILAND)
Maseru
LESOTHO
Bloemfontein

SOUTH AFRICA

Cape Town

The British Isles at the same scale.

Cape Town, South Africa.

The giant pyramids at Giza, Egypt.

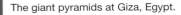

0 450 900 1350 1800 2250 km

Scale : One centimetre on this map is the same as 450 kilometres on the ground.

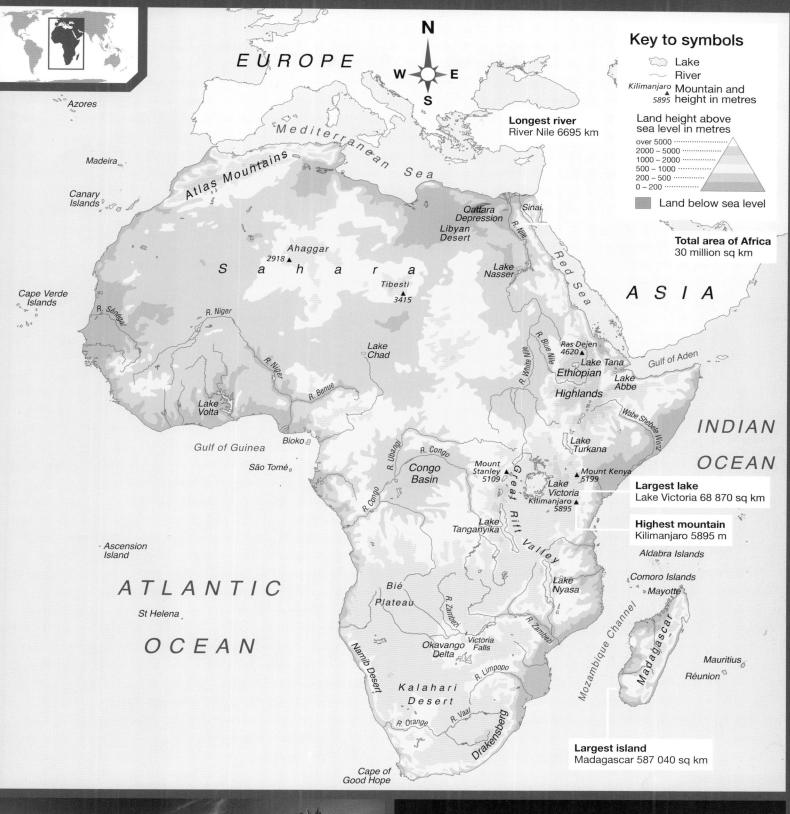

EUROPE

Azores

Madeira

Canary Islands

Mediterranean Sea

Atlas Mountains

Qattara Depression

Libyan Desert

Sinai

R. Nile

Ahaggar 2918 ▲

S a h a r a

Tibesti ▲ 3415

Lake Nasser

Red Sea

ASIA

Cape Verde Islands

R. Senegal

R. Niger

R. Niger

Lake Chad

R. Benue

Lake Volta

Bioko

Gulf of Guinea

São Tomé

R. Ubangi

R. Congo

Congo Basin

R. Congo

R. White Nile

R. Blue Nile

Ras Dejen 4620 ▲

Lake Tana

Ethiopian Highlands

Lake Abbe

Gulf of Aden

Wabe Shebele Wenz

Lake Turkana

Mount Stanley 5109 ▲

Mount Kenya 5199 ▲

Lake Victoria

Kilimanjaro ▲ 5895

Great Rift Valley

INDIAN OCEAN

Lake Tanganyika

Ascension Island

ATLANTIC

OCEAN

St Helena

Bié Plateau

R. Zambezi

Lake Nyasa

Aldabra Islands

Comoro Islands

Mayotte

Mozambique Channel

Madagascar

Okavango Delta

Victoria Falls

R. Zambezi

Namib Desert

Mauritius

Réunion

R. Limpopo

K a l a h a r i D e s e r t

R. Orange

R. Vaal

Drakensberg

Cape of Good Hope

Key to symbols

⬭ Lake

⎯ River

Kilimanjaro ▲ Mountain and
5895 height in metres

Land height above
sea level in metres

over 5000 ....
2000 – 5000 ....
1000 – 2000 ....
500 – 1000 ....
200 – 500 ....
0 – 200 ....

◼ Land below sea level

Longest river
River Nile 6695 km

Total area of Africa
30 million sq km

Largest lake
Lake Victoria 68 870 sq km

Highest mountain
Kilimanjaro 5895 m

Largest island
Madagascar 587 040 sq km

A Bedouin nomad in the Sahara Desert with his camels.

Kilimanjaro, an extinct volcano, is the highest mountain in Africa.

Scale : One centimetre on this map is the same as 450 kilometres on the ground.

A B C D

5

10° W   Málaga   0°   **Algiers**   Annaba Bizerte 10° E   Sicily   20° E   GRE
Tangier   Gibraltar (UK)   Oran   Sétif   Constantine   **Tunis**   **Valletta**   Mediterr
Tétouan   Chlef   Batna   Sousse   **MALTA**
Rabat   Fez   Oujda   Sidi Bel Abbès   Gafsa   Sfax
Casablanca   Meknès   Gulf of Gabès
MOROCCO   Touggourt   Gabès   **Tripoli**   Misratah
Marrakesh   Ghardaïa   Medenine   Benghazi
Jebel Toubkal   **High Atlas**   Saharan Atlas   **TUNISIA**   Sirte   Ajdabiy
4167   Béchar   Ghadāmis
Agadir   Atlas Mountains

20° W   30° N
Madeira (Portugal)
Funchal

Santa Cruz de Tenerife   Lanzarote
Tenerife   Las Palmas de Gran Canaria   Laayoune   Ksabi   **A L G E R I A**   **L I B Y A**
Canary Islands (Spain)   Gran Canaria   In Salah   Maradah

4   Tropic of Cancer   **Western Sahara**   Bir Mogreïn   Sabha
Administered by Morocco   **S**   Ghat
Dakhla   Choûm   Ahaggar   A   H   A   R
Mt Tahat   2918   Tibesti
Râs Nouâdhibou   Tamanrasset   Zouar
20° N   Nouâdhibou   Emi Koussi   3415

M A U R I T A N I A
Nouakchott
N   I   G   E   R
3   St-Louis   R. Sénégal   Timbuktu   Agadez   Koro Toro
Cap Vert   Thiès   Gao   **C H A D**
Dakar   **SENEGAL**   Kayes   **M A L I**   Nguigmi   Abéché
Banjul   Kaolack   Mopti   Maradi   Zinder   Lake Chad
THE GAMBIA   R. Gambia   R. Niger   R. Bani   Sokoto   **Ndjamena**
Koundâra   San   Katsina
Bissau   Bamako   **BURKINA FASO**   Dosso   Sokoto   Kano   Maiduguri
GUINEA BISSAU   Sikasso   **Ouagadougou**   R. Niger   Zaria   Garoua
GUINEA   Kankan   Bobo-   R. Black Volta   Kaduna   Kumo
10° N   Dioulasso   Jos   Kélo   Sarh
Conakry   **BENIN**   **CENTRAL A**
SIERRA LEONE   **Abuja**   Ngaoundéré   **REPU**
Freetown   R. White Volta   Parakou   **N I G E R I A**
Guéckédou   Tamale   Ilorin   Makurdi
CÔTE   Bouaké   **GHANA**   Ogbomoso   Bouar   Sibut
Daloa   **TOGO**   Ibadan   R. Benue
LIBERIA   **D'IVOIRE**   Kumasi   Benin City   **CAMEROON**   **Bangui**
Monrovia   **Yamoussoukro**   Lake Volta   Lagos   Enugu   Ngaoundéré
2   Abidjan   Cotonou   **Lomé**   Onitsha   Nkongsamba
Cape Palmas   **Accra**   **Porto-Novo**   Calabar   Mount Cameroon
Sekondi   Bight of Benin   Port Harcourt   4095   **Douala**
Gulf of Guinea   **EQUATORIAL GUINEA**   **Yaoundé**
Malabo
Bioko   **EQUATORIAL GUINEA**

Príncipe   Ouesso   Con
Bas
SÃO TOMÉ AND PRÍNCIPE   **São Tomé**   Mbandaka
São Tomé   **Libreville**   Lisa
Port-Gentil   **GABON**
0°   Equator   **ATLANTIC OCEAN**   Francecille   R. Congo

A   Bandundu   R. Kasai
1   Ponta do Sol   Pointe-   **Brazzaville**   **Kinshasa**   Ile
CAPE VERDE   Noire   R. Congo   R. Kwilu
Santiago   15° N
Praia
25° W   10° W   0°   10° E   20° E
B   C   D

0   200   400   600   800 km

Scale : One centimetre on this map is the same as 200 kilometres on the ground.

Algeria C4
Capital : Algiers

Benin C3
Capital : Porto-Novo

Burkina Faso B3
Capital : Ouagadougou

Cameroon D2
Capital : Yaoundé

Cape Verde A2
Capital : Praia

Central African Republic D2
Capital : Bangui

Chad D3
Capital : Ndjamena

Côte d'Ivoire B
Capital : Yamoussoukro

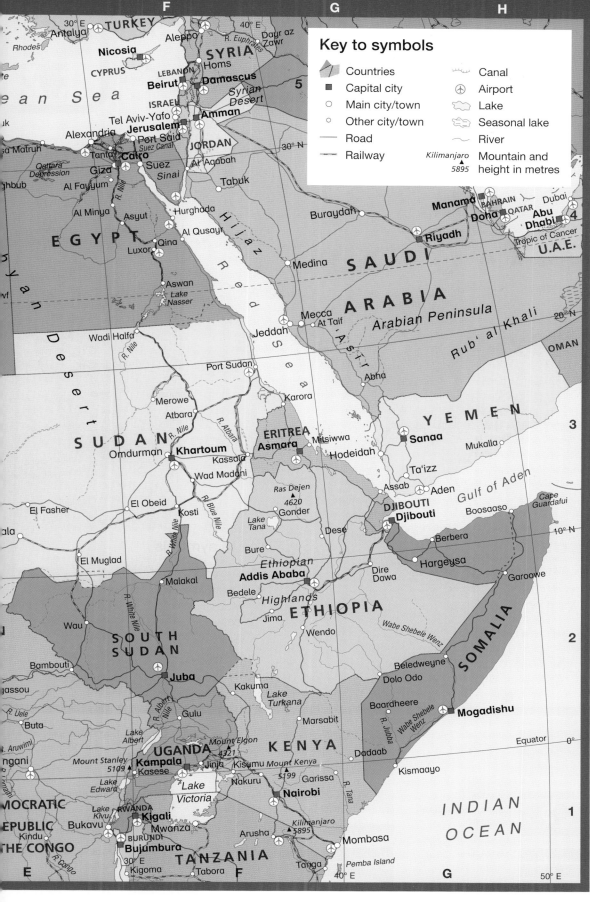

Key to symbols

Countries		Canal	
Capital city		Airport	
Main city/town		Lake	
Other city/town		Seasonal lake	
Road		River	
Railway		Kilimanjaro 5895	Mountain and height in metres

The Gambia A3
Capital : Banjul

Nigeria C2
Capital : Abuja

Ghana B2
Capital : Accra

São Tomé and Príncipe C2
Capital : São Tomé

Guinea A3
Capital : Conakry

Senegal A3
Capital : Dakar

Guinea-Bissau A3
Capital : Bissau

Sierra Leone A2
Capital : Freetown

Liberia A2
Capital : Monrovia

Somalia G2
Capital : Mogadishu

Libya D4
Capital : Tripoli

South Sudan E2
Capital : Juba

Mali B3
Capital : Bamako

Sudan E3
Capital : Khartoum

Mauritania A3
Capital : Nouakchott

Togo C2
Capital : Lomé

Morocco B5
Capital : Rabat

Tunisia C5
Capital : Tunis

Djibouti G3
Capital : Djibouti

Egypt E4
Capital : Cairo

Equatorial Guinea C2
Capital : Malabo

Eritrea F3
Capital : Asmara

Ethiopia F2
Capital : Addis Ababa

Gabon D1
Capital : Libreville

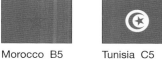

Niger C3
Capital : Niamey

Uganda F2
Capital : Kampala

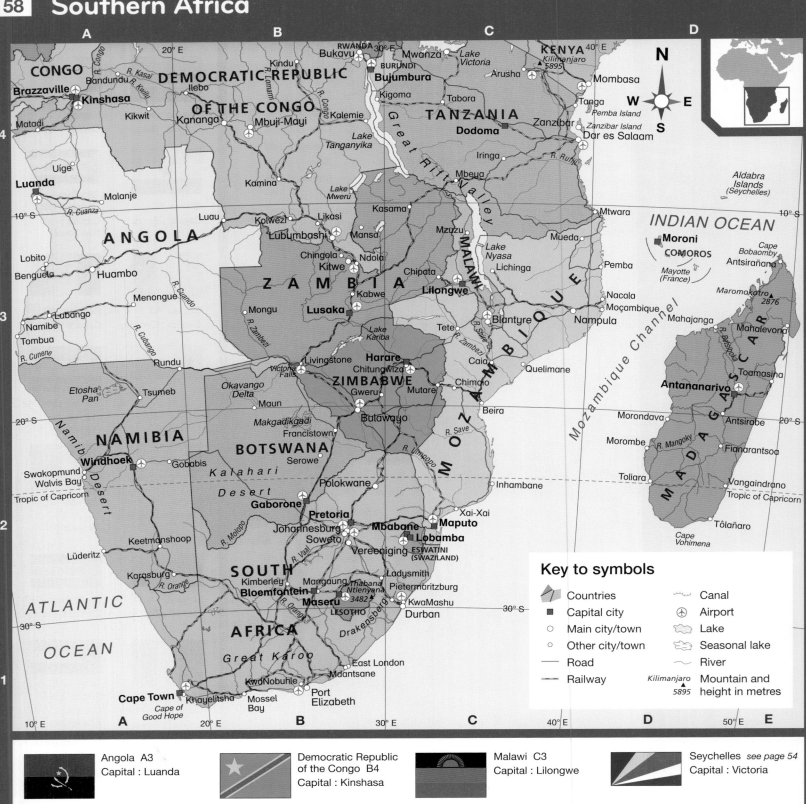

Key to symbols

Countries	Canal
Capital city	Airport
Main city/town	Lake
Other city/town	Seasonal lake
Road	River
Railway	Kilimanjaro 5895 — Mountain and height in metres

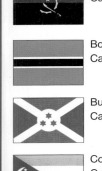 Angola A3
Capital : Luanda

 Botswana B2
Capital : Gaborone

Burundi B4
Capital : Bujumbura

 Comoros D3
Capital : Moroni

Congo A4
Capital : Brazzaville

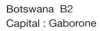 Democratic Republic of the Congo B4
Capital : Kinshasa

 Eswatini C2
Capital : Mbabane/ Lobamba

 Kenya C4
Capital : Nairobi

 Lesotho B2
Capital : Maseru

Madagascar D2
Capital : Antananarivo

 Malawi C3
Capital : Lilongwe

Mauritius *see page 54*
Capital : Port Louis

 Mozambique C2
Capital : Maputo

 Namibia A2
Capital : Windhoek

 Rwanda B4
Capital : Kigali

 Seychelles *see page 54*
Capital : Victoria

 South Africa B2
Capital : Pretoria/Cape Town/ Bloemfontein

 Tanzania C4
Capital : Dodoma

 Zambia B3
Capital : Lusaka

 Zimbabwe B3
Capital : Harare

0   200   400   600   800 km

Scale : One centimetre on this map is the same as 200 kilometres on the ground.

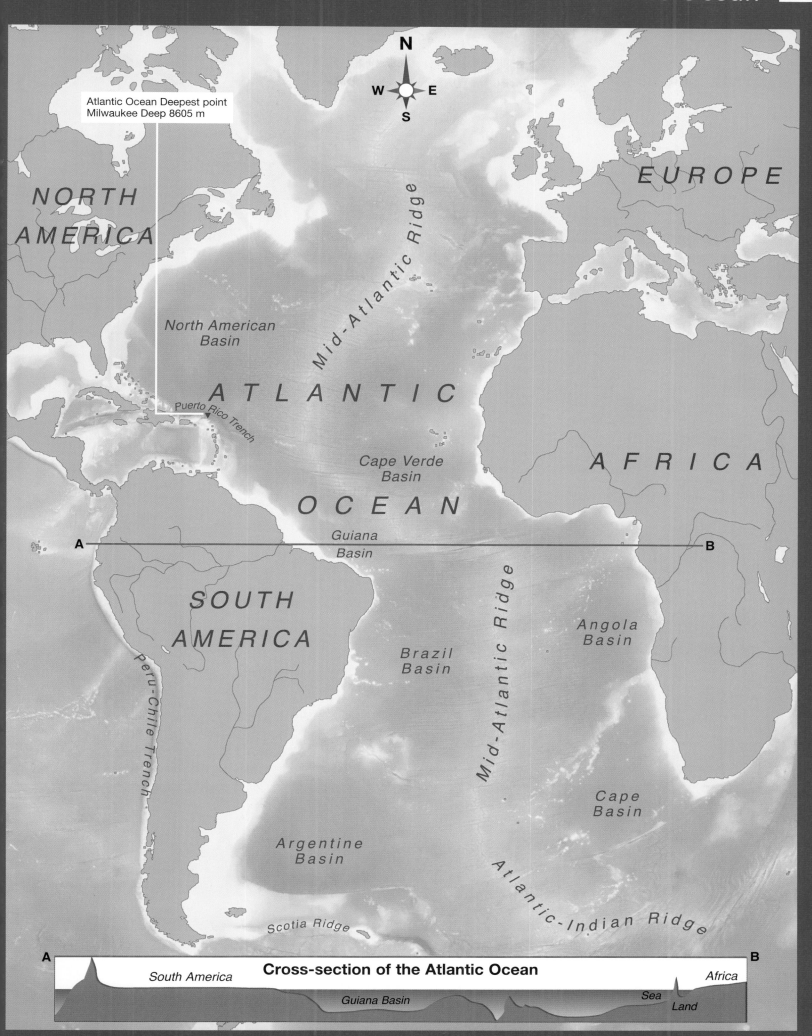

Atlantic Ocean Deepest point
Milwaukee Deep 8605 m

NORTH
AMERICA

EUROPE

Mid-Atlantic Ridge

North American
Basin

ATLANTIC

Puerto Rico Trench

AFRICA

Cape Verde
Basin

OCEAN

Guiana
Basin

A ———————————————————————————— B

SOUTH
AMERICA

Peru-Chile Trench

Brazil
Basin

Mid-Atlantic Ridge

Angola
Basin

Cape
Basin

Argentine
Basin

Scotia Ridge

Atlantic-Indian Ridge

A **Cross-section of the Atlantic Ocean** B

South America

Africa

Guiana Basin

Sea
Land

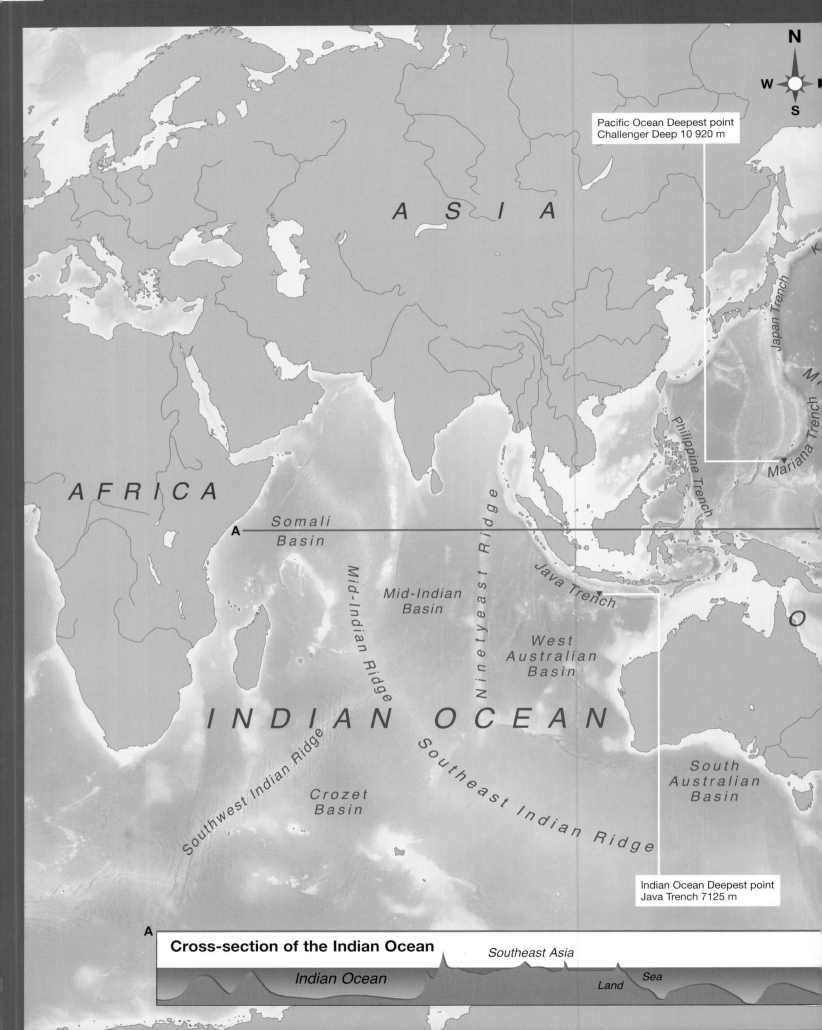

N
W   E
S

Pacific Ocean Deepest point
Challenger Deep 10 920 m

ASIA

Japan Trench

Mariana Trench

Philippine Trench

AFRICA

A   Somali
Basin

Mid-Indian Ridge

Mid-Indian
Basin

Ninetyeast Ridge

Java Trench

West
Australian
Basin

O

INDIAN OCEAN

Southwest Indian Ridge

Southeast Indian Ridge

Crozet
Basin

South
Australian
Basin

Indian Ocean Deepest point
Java Trench 7125 m

A

Cross-section of the Indian Ocean

Southeast Asia

Indian Ocean

Land   Sea

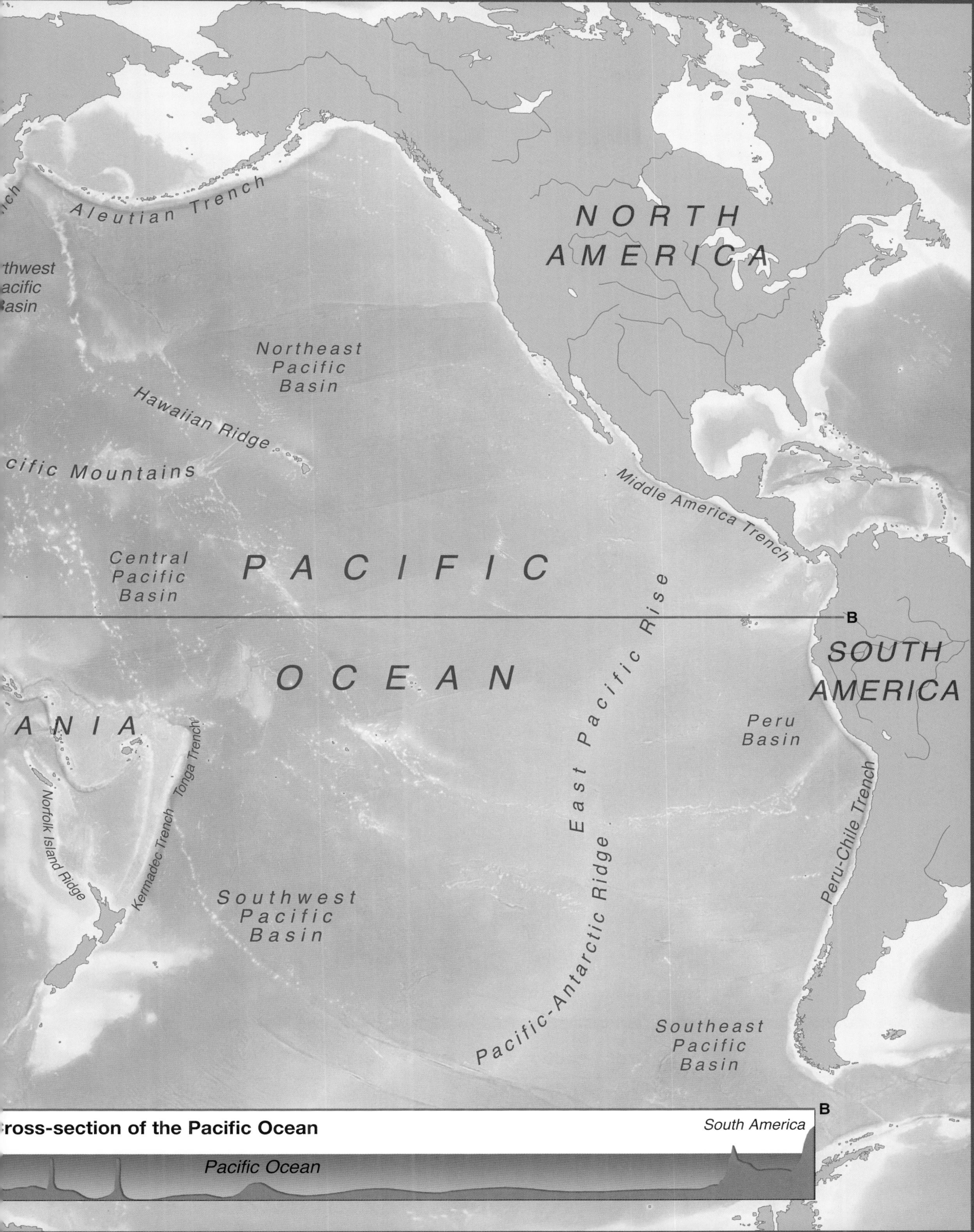

NORTH AMERICA

Aleutian Trench

rthwest acific Basin

Northeast Pacific Basin

Hawaiian Ridge

cific Mountains

Central Pacific Basin

PACIFIC

OCEAN

Middle America Trench

SOUTH AMERICA

Peru Basin

East Pacific Rise

ANIA

Norfolk Island Ridge

Kermadec Trench

Tonga Trench

Southwest Pacific Basin

Pacific-Antarctic Ridge

Southeast Pacific Basin

Peru-Chile Trench

B

B

ross-section of the Pacific Ocean

South America

Pacific Ocean

Key to symbols

～ River
〰 Lake
▢ Ice cap
▢ Polar pack ice
▢ Drifting ice

Land height above sea level in metres

over 2000
1000 – 2000
500 – 1000
200 – 500
0 – 200

The British Isles at the same scale.

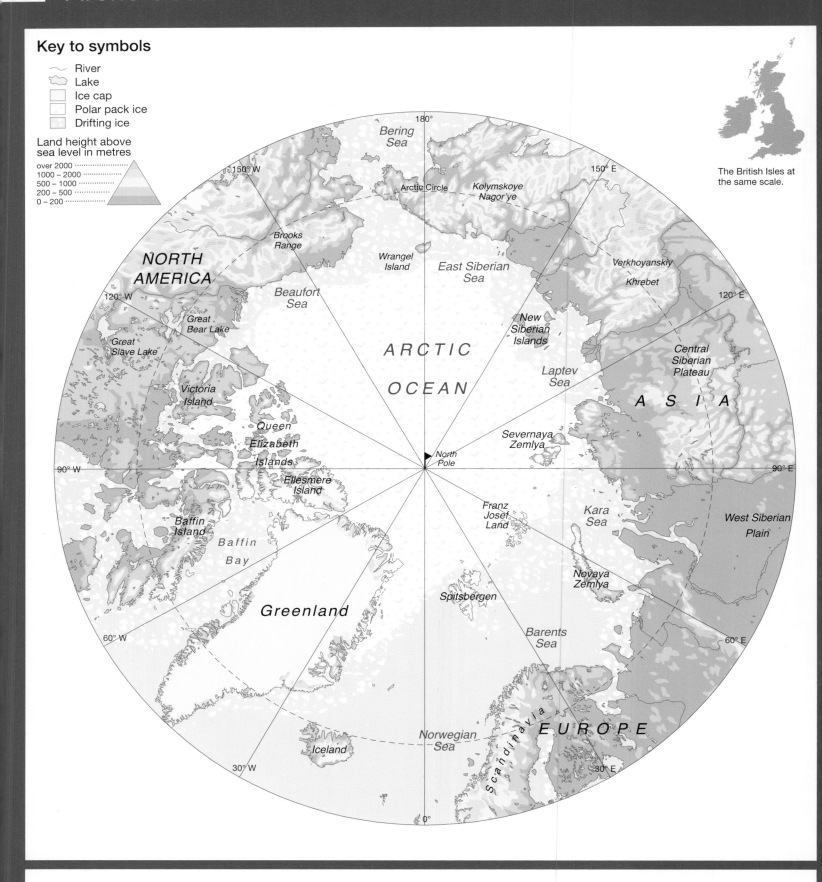

Bering Sea

180°

150° W

Arctic Circle

Kolymskoye Nagor'ye

150° E

Brooks Range

Wrangel Island

East Siberian Sea

Verkhoyanskiy Khrebet

NORTH AMERICA

120° W

Beaufort Sea

120° E

Great Bear Lake

New Siberian Islands

Central Siberian Plateau

Great Slave Lake

A S I A

ARCTIC

Victoria Island

OCEAN

Laptev Sea

Queen Elizabeth Islands

Severnaya Zemlya

90° W

North Pole

90° E

Ellesmere Island

West Siberian Plain

Baffin Island

Franz Josef Land

Kara Sea

Baffin Bay

Spitsbergen

Novaya Zemlya

Greenland

60° W

Barents Sea

60° E

Norwegian Sea

E U R O P E

30° W

Iceland

Scandinavia

30° E

0°

Cross-section of the Arctic Ocean

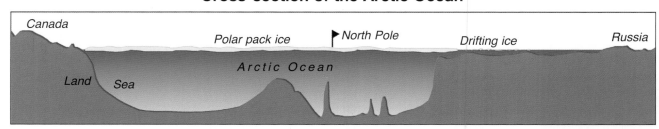

Canada

Polar pack ice

▶ North Pole

Drifting ice

Russia

Land   Sea

Arctic Ocean

---

0   500   1000   1500   2000 km

Scale : One centimetre on this map is the same as 350 kilometres on the ground.

Manned bases in the Antarctic Peninsula

① Comandante Ferraz (Brazil)
② King Sejong (South Korea)
③ Artigas (Uruguay)
④ Eduardo Frei (Chile)
⑤ Bellingshausen (Russia)
⑥ Great Wall (China)
⑦ Carlini (Argentina)
⑧ Henryk Arctowski (Poland)
⑨ Bernardo O'Higgins (Chile)
⑩ San Martin (Argentina)

Key to symbols

- Ice shelf
- Ice cap
- Polar pack ice
- Drifting ice

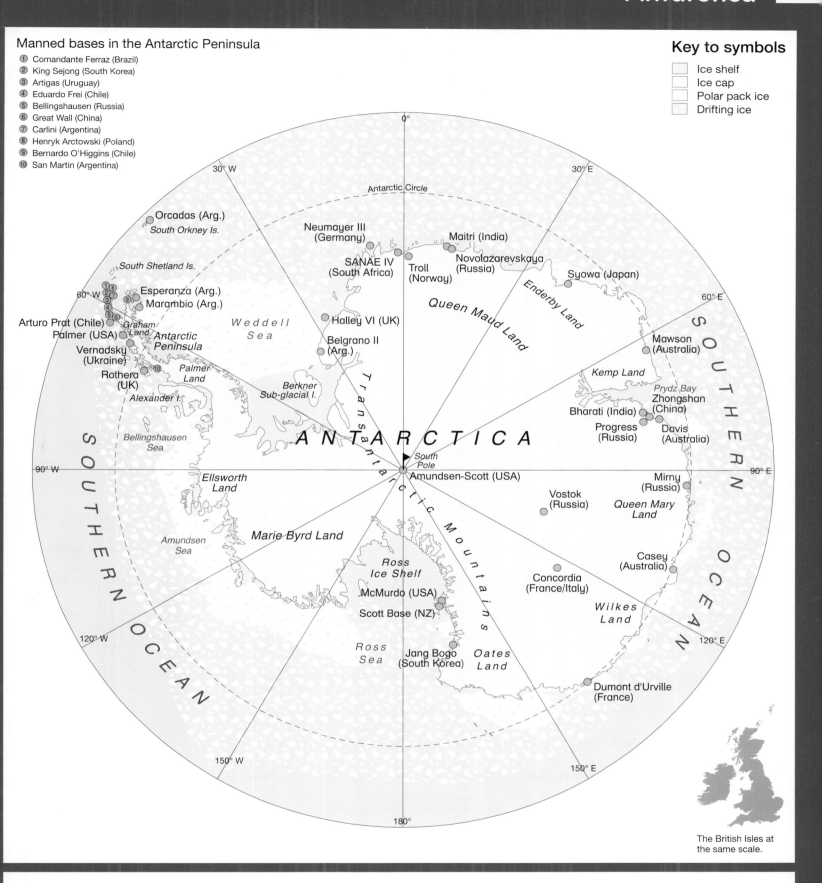

The British Isles at the same scale.

Cross-section of Antarctica

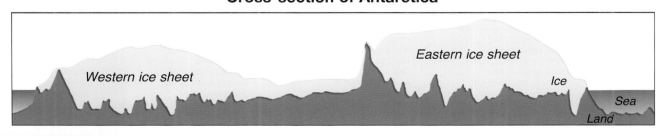

Western ice sheet

Eastern ice sheet

Ice

Sea

Land

500   1000   1500   2000 km

Scale : One centimetre on this map is the same as 350 kilometres on the ground.

place name — grid code
Cairo *capital* 57 F5
page number
cities and towns are shown in green

place name — grid code
Tyne *river* 22 D4
page number
water features are shown in blue

place name — grid code
Italy *country* 28 G3
page number
countries and states are shown in red

place name — grid code
Corsica *island* 28 F3
page number
physical features are shown in black